Fiat LITURGICAL PLANNER

2024

Copyright © 2023 by Liturgy of the Home.
Printed in the United States of America. All rights reserved.

No part of this book may be reproduced, stored in a retrieval system, or transmitted in any form, or by any means, electronic, mechanical, photocopying, or otherwise, without the prior written permission of the publisher, except by a reviewer, who may quote brief passages in a review.

Sophia Institute Press
Box 5284, Manchester, NH 03108
1-800-888-9344
www.SophiaInstitute.com
Sophia Institute Press® is a registered trademark of Sophia Institute.

ISBN 978-1-64413-894-6

Personal Information

NAME

PHONE

EMAIL

ADDRESS

Important Contacts

NAME

PHONE

EMAIL

ADDRESS

NAME

PHONE

EMAIL

ADDRESS

NAME

PHONE

EMAIL

ADDRESS

NAME

PHONE

EMAIL

ADDRESS

NAME

PHONE

EMAIL

ADDRESS

ILLUSTRATED LITURGICAL PLANNER

JANUARY 2024 – DECEMBER 2024

This planner is the work of Liturgy of the Home, a small family apostolate, and is not backed by any official Catholic office or representative. The feasts in the planner are placed according to the General Roman Calendar of 1962. All Sundays, feasts, vigils, and ferias with their own Mass readings are illustrated. On days that do not have their own Mass readings, a Scripture verse is shown instead, inspired by either the Sunday readings or another important feast that week.

We hope that the art, Scripture, prayers, and quotations in these pages enrich your life and keep you close to the Faith in the midst of your day-to-day. Share how you use the planner on Instagram with #thefiatplanner. We would love to see it in your hands!

INTRODUCTION TO THE LITURGICAL YEAR

The liturgical year operates in two cycles: the Temporal Cycle and the Sanctoral Cycle. The Temporal Cycle follows the events in the life of Christ, and the Sanctoral Cycle celebrates the feasts of the saints. The Temporal Cycle creates greater seasons within the Church. These seasons give the liturgical year its life, the ebb and flow of times of sadness and times of rejoicing. Within these greater seasons, the Sanctoral Cycle gives us smaller occasions for fasting and feasting. The Church uses colors to symbolize these different periods: purple for times of penance; green, representing life, for the times after Epiphany and Pentecost; white for seasons of triumph and glory; red for God's love and for martyrdom; rose for joy; and black for mourning.

Keys to Use

FASTING AND ABSTINENCE

The fishes that represent the various laws of fasting and abstinence follow the 1962 laws, with an inversion of the colors whenever fasting or abstinence are still required under current Church law. This planner does not include any indication to the current law of mandatory penance that replaces most Fridays' traditional abstinence. See the chart to the right.

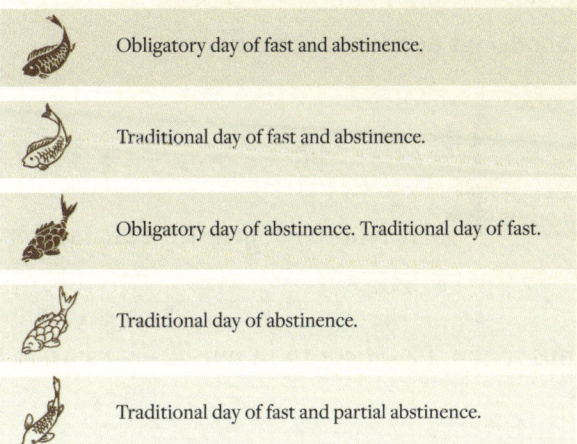

CLASSES OF FEASTS, LITURGICAL COLORS, AND MORE

The classes of feasts are indicated by Roman numerals on the weekly spread, on a color banner showing the liturgical color of the feast. On the monthly spread, the liturgical colors are given for the first- and second-class feasts, with the first-class feasts given in capital letters. Holy Days of Obligation, along with the first Friday and Saturday of the month, are indicated by small icons both in the weekly and monthly spread.

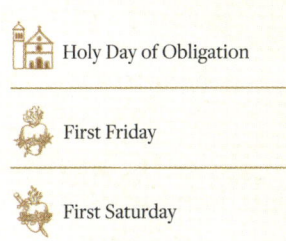

Major Feast Days

THE CIRCUMCISION / January 1

EPIPHANY / January 6

ASH WEDNESDAY / February 14

PASSION SUNDAY / March 17

ST. JOSEPH, SPOUSE OF THE B.V.M. / March 19

PALM SUNDAY / March 24

HOLY THURSDAY / March 28

GOOD FRIDAY / March 29

HOLY SATURDAY / March 30

EASTER SUNDAY / March 31

THE ANNUNCIATION / April 8

ST. JOSEPH THE WORKMAN / May 1

THE ASCENSION OF OUR LORD / May 9

VIGIL OF PENTECOST / May 18

PENTECOST SUNDAY / May 19

TRINITY SUNDAY / May 26

CORPUS CHRISTI / May 30

SACRED HEART OF JESUS / June 7

NATIVITY OF ST. JOHN THE BAPTIST / June 24

STS. PETER AND PAUL / June 29

THE MOST PRECIOUS BLOOD / July 1

THE ASSUMPTION OF OUR LADY / August 15

THE DEDICATION OF ST. MICHAEL THE ARCHANGEL / September 29

CHRIST THE KING / October 27

ALL SAINTS / November 1

ALL SOULS / November 2

THE IMMACULATE CONCEPTION / December 8

VIGIL OF THE NATIVITY / December 24

THE NATIVITY OF OUR LORD / December 25

Angelus Chant

℟. Angelus Domini nuntiavit Mariae,
℣. Et concepit de Spiritu Sancto.

Ave María, grá-ti-a pléna, Dómi-nus técum. Benedicta tu in mu-li-é-ribus, et benedictus fructus ventris tu-i, Je-sus. Sancta Ma-ri-a, Ma-ter De-i, ora pro no-bis pecca-to-ri-bus, nunc, et in ho-ra mortis nostrae. Amen.

℟. Ecce ancilla Domini,
℣. Fiat mihi secundum verbum tuum.
Ave Maria…

℟. Et Verbum caro factum est.
℣. Et habitavit in nobis.
Ave Maria…

℟. Ora pro nobis, sancta Dei Genitrix.
℣. Ut digni efficiamur promissionibus Christi.

Oremus.
Gratiam tuam, quaesumus, Domine, mentibus nostris infunde; ut, qui, angelo nuntiante, Christi Filii tui incarnationem cognovimus, per passionem ejus et crucem, ad resurrectionis gloriam perducamur. Per eumdem Christum Dominum nostrum.
℟. Amen.

The angel of the Lord declared unto Mary,
And she conceived of the Holy Spirit.
Hail Mary…

Behold the handmaid of the Lord,
Be it done unto me according to your word.
Hail Mary…

And the Word was made flesh,
And dwelt among us.
Hail Mary…

Pray for us, O Holy Mother of God,
That we may be made worthy of the promises of Christ.

Let us pray. Pour forth, we beseech You, O Lord, Your grace into our hearts, that we, to whom the Incarnation of Christ, Your Son, was made known by the message of an angel, may by His Passion and Cross be brought to the glory of His Resurrection, through the same Christ Our Lord. Amen.

Personal Goals

PHYSICAL

- ☐ ....
- ☐ ....
- ☐ ....

SPIRITUAL

- ☐ ....
- ☐ ....
- ☐ ....

INTELLECTUAL

- ☐ ....
- ☐ ....
- ☐ ....

FINANCIAL

- ☐ ....
- ☐ ....
- ☐ ....

WORK

- ☐ ....
- ☐ ....
- ☐ ....

RELATIONSHIPS

- ☐ ....
- ☐ ....
- ☐ ....

Reading List

TITLE AND AUTHOR	STARTED ON...	FINISHED ON...
	/ /	/ /
	/ /	/ /
	/ /	/ /
	/ /	/ /
	/ /	/ /
	/ /	/ /
	/ /	/ /
	/ /	/ /
	/ /	/ /
	/ /	/ /
	/ /	/ /
	/ /	/ /
	/ /	/ /
	/ /	/ /
	/ /	/ /
	/ /	/ /
	/ /	/ /
	/ /	/ /
	/ /	/ /
	/ /	/ /
	/ /	/ /
	/ /	/ /

"Don't consider me too demanding if I ask you once again to set great store by holy books and read them as much as you can. This spiritual reading is as necessary to you as the air you breathe."
ST. PADRE PIO

"It is very useful for those who minister the word of God, or give themselves up to prayer, to read the works of authors whose names begin with S, such as Saint Augustine, Saint Bernard, etc."
ST. PHILIP NERI

"Spiritual reading is a sovereign remedy against evil thoughts."
ST. JEROME

"The reading of the lives of the Saints contributes greatly to infuse courage into the soul."
ST. ALPHONSUS LIGUORI

 Reading List

TITLE AND AUTHOR	STARTED ON . . .	FINISHED ON . . .
	/ /	/ /
	/ /	/ /
	/ /	/ /
	/ /	/ /
	/ /	/ /
	/ /	/ /
	/ /	/ /
	/ /	/ /
	/ /	/ /
	/ /	/ /
	/ /	/ /
	/ /	/ /
	/ /	/ /
	/ /	/ /
	/ /	/ /
	/ /	/ /
	/ /	/ /
	/ /	/ /
	/ /	/ /
	/ /	/ /
	/ /	/ /
	/ /	/ /
	/ /	/ /

"Spiritual reading is the food of the soul, which renders it dauntless and strong against all temptation, which prompts it with holy thoughts and ardent desires for Heaven, which enlightens the mind, strengthens the will, and gives comfort in all afflictions, which, in conclusion, procures that holy joy that is found in God alone."

ST. AMBROSE

"Only God knows the good that can come about by reading one good Catholic book."

ST. JOHN BOSCO

"Read with attention and application of mind and heart."

ST. JOHN EUDES

"He who wishes often to be with God ought to pray frequently and read pious books."

ST. AUGUSTINE

January
The Month of the Holy Name

PRAYER FOR JANUARY

Jesus, the very thought of Thee with sweetness fills the breast! Yet sweeter far Thy face to see and in Thy presence rest. No voice can sing, no heart can frame, nor can the memory find, a sweeter sound than Jesus' name, the Savior of mankind.

—EXCERPT FROM A PRAYER BY ST. BERNARD OF CLAIRVAUX

GOALS AND NOTES

January 2024
The Month of the Holy Name

DECEMBER 2023

S	M	T	W	T	F	S
					1	2
3	4	5	6	7	8	9
10	11	12	13	14	15	16
17	18	19	20	21	22	23
24	25	26	27	28	29	30
31						

FEBRUARY 2024

S	M	T	W	T	F	S
				1	2	3
4	5	6	7	8	9	10
11	12	13	14	15	16	17
18	19	20	21	22	23	24
25	26	27	28	29		

SUNDAY *Resurrection & Trinity*	MONDAY *Holy Spirit*	TUESDAY *Holy Angels*	WEDNESDAY *St. Joseph*
	1 New Year's Day THE CIRCUMCISION	**2** Holy Name of Jesus	**3**
7 Holy Family of Jesus, Mary, and Joseph	**8**	**9**	**10**
14 Second Sunday after Epiphany	**15** Martin Luther King Jr. Birthday St. Paul, the First Hermit	**16** St. Marcellus I	**17** St. Anthony the Great
21 Third Sunday after Epiphany	**22** Day of Prayer for the Legal Protection of Unborn Children Sts. Vincent and Anastasius	**23** St. Raymond of Peñafort	**24** St. Timothy
28 Septuagesima Sunday	**29** St. Francis de Sales	**30** St. Martina of Rome	**31** St. John Bosco

"If thou art bound down by sickness, if sorrows weary thee, if thou art trembling with fear, invoke the name of Jesus."
ST. LAWRENCE JUSTINIAN

THURSDAY *The Eucharist*	FRIDAY *Christ's Passion*	SATURDAY *The Blessed Virgin Mary*
4	5	6 EPIPHANY
11	12	13 The Baptism of Our Lord
18	19	20 Sts. Fabian and Sebastian
25 The Conversion of St. Paul	26 St. Polycarp	27 St. John Chrysostom

NOTES

Week of December 31 to January 6

"Arise, all ye nobles and peasants; Mary invites all, rich and poor, just and sinners, to enter the cave of Bethlehem, to adore and to kiss the feet of her newborn Son."

ST. ALPHONSUS LIGUORI

WEEKLY GOALS

HABIT TRACKER

S M T W T F S

THIS WEEK

MEAL PLAN

Sunday

Monday

Tuesday

Wednesday

Thursday

Friday

Saturday

THINGS TO REMEMBER

SUNDAY, DECEMBER 31 / Seventh Day in the Octave of Christmas / New Year's Eve

MONDAY, JANUARY 1 / The Circumcision / New Year's Day / *Holy Day of Obligation*

TUESDAY, JANUARY 2 / Holy Name of Jesus

WEDNESDAY, JANUARY 3 / Feria of Christmas

"And after eight days were accomplished, that the child should be circumcised, his name was called JESUS."

LUKE 2:21

☐ **THURSDAY, JANUARY 4** / Feria of Christmas

> "In the name of Jesus every knee should bow, of those that are in heaven, on earth, and under the earth."
>
> **PHILIPPIANS 2:10**

☐ **FRIDAY, JANUARY 5** / Feria of Christmas / *First Friday*

> "All the nations thou hast made shall come and adore before thee, O Lord: and they shall glorify thy name."
>
> **PSALMS 85:9**

☐ **SATURDAY, JANUARY 6** / Epiphany / *First Saturday*

CALL / EMAIL / FOLLOW-UP

JANUARY 2024

S	M	T	W	T	F	S
	1	2	3	4	5	6
7	8	9	10	11	12	13
14	15	16	17	18	19	20
21	22	23	24	25	26	27
28	29	30	31			

FEBRUARY 2024

S	M	T	W	T	F	S
				1	2	3
4	5	6	7	8	9	10
11	12	13	14	15	16	17
18	19	20	21	22	23	24
25	26	27	28	29		

Week of January 7–13

"Whatever you do for your family, your children, your husband, your wife, you do for God."
MOTHER TERESA

WEEKLY GOALS

HABIT TRACKER

S M T W T F S

THIS WEEK

MEAL PLAN

Sunday

Monday

Tuesday

Wednesday

Thursday

Friday

Saturday

THINGS TO REMEMBER

	SUNDAY, JANUARY 7 / Holy Family of Jesus, Mary, and Joseph

"He said to them: How is it that you sought me? did you not know, that I must be about my father's business?"

LUKE 2:49

	MONDAY, JANUARY 8 / Feria of Epiphany

"All that heard him were astonished at his wisdom and his answers. And seeing him, they wondered."

LUKE 2:47–48

	TUESDAY, JANUARY 9 / Feria of Epiphany

"The father of the just rejoiceth greatly.... Let thy father, and thy mother be joyful, and let her rejoice that bore thee."

PROVERBS 23:24–25

	WEDNESDAY, JANUARY 10 / Feria of Epiphany

☐ **THURSDAY, JANUARY 11** / Feria of Epiphany

> "Let the word of Christ dwell in you abundantly, in all wisdom: teaching and admonishing one another in psalms, hymns, and spiritual canticles."
>
> **COLOSSIANS 3:16**

☐ **FRIDAY, JANUARY 12** / Feria of Epiphany

> "He upon whom thou shalt see the Spirit descending, and remaining upon him, he it is that baptizeth with the Holy Ghost."
>
> **JOHN 1:33**

☐ **SATURDAY, JANUARY 13** / The Baptism of Our Lord

CALL / EMAIL / FOLLOW-UP

JANUARY 2024

S	M	T	W	T	F	S
	1	2	3	4	5	6
7	8	9	10	11	12	13
14	15	16	17	18	19	20
21	22	23	24	25	26	27
28	29	30	31			

FEBRUARY 2024

S	M	T	W	T	F	S
				1	2	3
4	5	6	7	8	9	10
11	12	13	14	15	16	17
18	19	20	21	22	23	24
25	26	27	28	29		

Week of January 14–20

"To say that God turns away from the sinful is like saying that the sun hides from the blind."
ST. ANTHONY THE GREAT

WEEKLY GOALS

HABIT TRACKER

S M T W T F S

THIS WEEK

MEAL PLAN

Sunday

Monday

Tuesday

Wednesday

Thursday

Friday

Saturday

THINGS TO REMEMBER

SUNDAY, JANUARY 14 / Second Sunday after Epiphany

MONDAY, JANUARY 15 / St. Paul, the First Hermit / Martin Luther King Jr. Birthday

TUESDAY, JANUARY 16 / St. Marcellus I

WEDNESDAY, JANUARY 17 / St. Anthony the Great

IV THURSDAY, JANUARY 18 / Feria

> "Bless the Lord, all ye his angels: you that are mighty in strength, and execute his word, hearkening to the voice of his orders."
>
> **PSALMS 102:20**

IV FRIDAY, JANUARY 19 / Feria

> "Be glad in the Lord, and rejoice, ye just, and glory, all ye right of heart."
>
> **PSALMS 31:11**

III SATURDAY, JANUARY 20 / Sts. Fabian and Sebastian

CALL / EMAIL / FOLLOW-UP

JANUARY 2024

S	M	T	W	T	F	S
	1	2	3	4	5	6
7	8	9	10	11	12	13
14	15	16	17	18	19	20
21	22	23	24	25	26	27
28	29	30	31			

FEBRUARY 2024

S	M	T	W	T	F	S
				1	2	3
4	5	6	7	8	9	10
11	12	13	14	15	16	17
18	19	20	21	22	23	24
25	26	27	28	29		

Week of January 21–27

"But first I want you to tell me this: do you know the power of love? Christ passed over all the marvelous works which were to be performed by the apostles and said, 'By this shall men know that ye are my disciples, if ye love one another.'"
ST. JOHN CHRYSOSTOM

WEEKLY GOALS

HABIT TRACKER

S M T W T F S

THIS WEEK

MEAL PLAN

Sunday

Monday

Tuesday

Wednesday

Thursday

Friday

Saturday

THINGS TO REMEMBER

SUNDAY, JANUARY 21 / Third Sunday after Epiphany

MONDAY, JANUARY 22 / Sts. Vincent and Anastasius / Day of Prayer for the Legal Protection of Unborn Children

TUESDAY, JANUARY 23 / St. Raymond of Peñafort

WEDNESDAY, JANUARY 24 / St. Timothy

THURSDAY, JANUARY 25 / The Conversion of St. Paul

- [ ] ....
- [ ] ....
- [ ] ....
- [ ] ....
- [ ] ....
- [ ] ....
- [ ] ....
- [ ] ....
- [ ] ....
- [ ] ....

FRIDAY, JANUARY 26 / St. Polycarp

- [ ] ....
- [ ] ....
- [ ] ....
- [ ] ....
- [ ] ....
- [ ] ....
- [ ] ....
- [ ] ....
- [ ] ....
- [ ] ....

SATURDAY, JANUARY 27 / St. John Chrysostom

- [ ] ....
- [ ] ....
- [ ] ....
- [ ] ....
- [ ] ....
- [ ] ....
- [ ] ....
- [ ] ....
- [ ] ....
- [ ] ....

CALL / EMAIL / FOLLOW-UP

JANUARY 2024

S	M	T	W	T	F	S
	1	2	3	4	5	6
7	8	9	10	11	12	13
14	15	16	17	18	19	20
21	22	23	24	25	26	27
28	29	30	31			

FEBRUARY 2024

S	M	T	W	T	F	S
				1	2	3
4	5	6	7	8	9	10
11	12	13	14	15	16	17
18	19	20	21	22	23	24
25	26	27	28	29		

February
The Month of the Holy Family

PRAYER FOR FEBRUARY

Grant us, O Lord Jesus, faithfully to imitate the examples of Thy Holy Family, so that in the hour of our death, in the company of Thy glorious Virgin Mother and St. Joseph, we may deserve to be received by Thee into eternal tabernacles. Amen.

–PRE-1968 INDULGENCE OF THREE YEARS

GOALS AND NOTES

February 2024
The Month of the Holy Family

JANUARY 2024						
S	M	T	W	T	F	S
	1	2	3	4	5	6
7	8	9	10	11	12	13
14	15	16	17	18	19	20
21	22	23	24	25	26	27
28	29	30	31			

MARCH 2024						
S	M	T	W	T	F	S
					1	2
3	4	5	6	7	8	9
10	11	12	13	14	15	16
17	18	19	20	21	22	23
24	25	26	27	28	29	30
31						

SUNDAY *Resurrection & Trinity*	MONDAY *Holy Spirit*	TUESDAY *Holy Angels*	WEDNESDAY *St. Joseph*
4 Sexagesima Sunday	**5** St. Agatha	**6** St. Titus	**7** St. Romuald
11 Quinquagesima Sunday	**12** Seven Holy Servite Founders	**13** Shrove Tuesday	**14** Valentine's Day ASH WEDNESDAY
18 FIRST SUNDAY OF LENT	**19** President's Day	**20**	**21** Ember Wednesday of Lent
25 SECOND SUNDAY OF LENT	**26**	**27**	**28**

> "The family is the basis in the Lord's plan and all the forces of evil aim to demolish it. Uphold your families and guard them against the grudges of the evil one, by the Presence of God."
>
> ST. CHARBEL MAKHLOUF OLM

THURSDAY *The Eucharist*	FRIDAY *Christ's Passion*	SATURDAY *The Blessed Virgin Mary*	NOTES
1 St. Ignatius of Antioch	**2** The Purification of the B.V.M.	**3**	....
8 St. John of Matha	**9** St. Cyril of Alexandria	**10** St. Scholastica	....
15	**16**	**17**	....
22 Chair of St. Peter	**23** Ember Friday of Lent	**24** St. Matthias	....
29			....

Week of January 28–February 3

"We do not go to Holy Communion because we are good; we go to become good."
ST. JOHN BOSCO

WEEKLY GOALS

HABIT TRACKER

S M T W T F S

THIS WEEK

MEAL PLAN

Sunday

Monday

Tuesday

Wednesday

Thursday

Friday

Saturday

THINGS TO REMEMBER

SUNDAY, JANUARY 28 / Septuagesima Sunday

MONDAY, JANUARY 29 / St. Francis de Sales

TUESDAY, JANUARY 30 / St. Martina of Rome

WEDNESDAY, JANUARY 31 / St. John Bosco

THURSDAY, FEBRUARY 1 / St. Ignatius of Antioch

FRIDAY, FEBRUARY 2 / The Purification of the B.V.M. / *First Friday*

SATURDAY, FEBRUARY 3 / Our Lady on Saturday / *First Saturday*

CALL / EMAIL / FOLLOW-UP

FEBRUARY 2024

S	M	T	W	T	F	S
				1	2	3
4	5	6	7	8	9	10
11	12	13	14	15	16	17
18	19	20	21	22	23	24
25	26	27	28	29		

MARCH 2024

S	M	T	W	T	F	S
					1	2
3	4	5	6	7	8	9
10	11	12	13	14	15	16
17	18	19	20	21	22	23
24	25	26	27	28	29	30
31						

Week of February 4–10

"Indeed the mystery of Christ runs the risk of being disbelieved precisely because it is so incredibly wonderful."
ST. CYRIL OF ALEXANDRIA

WEEKLY GOALS

- [ ]
- [ ]
- [ ]
- [ ]
- [ ]
- [ ]
- [ ]
- [ ]
- [ ]

HABIT TRACKER

	S	M	T	W	T	F	S
_____	○	○	○	○	○	○	○
_____	○	○	○	○	○	○	○
_____	○	○	○	○	○	○	○
_____	○	○	○	○	○	○	○
_____	○	○	○	○	○	○	○
_____	○	○	○	○	○	○	○
_____	○	○	○	○	○	○	○
_____	○	○	○	○	○	○	○

THIS WEEK

- [ ]
- [ ]
- [ ]
- [ ]
- [ ]
- [ ]
- [ ]
- [ ]
- [ ]
- [ ]
- [ ]
- [ ]
- [ ]
- [ ]
- [ ]
- [ ]
- [ ]
- [ ]
- [ ]
- [ ]

MEAL PLAN

Sunday

Monday

Tuesday

Wednesday

Thursday

Friday

Saturday

THINGS TO REMEMBER

II   **SUNDAY, FEBRUARY 4** / Sexagesima Sunday

-
-
-
-
-
-
-
-
-
-
-
-

III   **MONDAY, FEBRUARY 5** / St. Agatha

-
-
-
-
-
-
-
-
-
-
-
-

III   **TUESDAY, FEBRUARY 6** / St. Titus

-
-
-
-
-
-
-
-
-
-
-
-

III   **WEDNESDAY, FEBRUARY 7** / St. Romuald

-
-
-
-
-
-
-
-
-

THURSDAY, FEBRUARY 8 / St. John of Matha

- ☐ ....
- ☐ ....
- ☐ ....
- ☐ ....
- ☐ ....
- ☐ ....
- ☐ ....
- ☐ ....
- ☐ ....
- ☐ ....

FRIDAY, FEBRUARY 9 / St. Cyril of Alexandria

- ☐ ....
- ☐ ....
- ☐ ....
- ☐ ....
- ☐ ....
- ☐ ....
- ☐ ....
- ☐ ....
- ☐ ....
- ☐ ....

SATURDAY, FEBRUARY 10 / St. Scholastica

- ☐ ....
- ☐ ....
- ☐ ....
- ☐ ....
- ☐ ....
- ☐ ....
- ☐ ....
- ☐ ....
- ☐ ....
- ☐ ....

CALL / EMAIL / FOLLOW-UP

FEBRUARY 2024

S	M	T	W	T	F	S
				1	2	3
4	5	6	7	8	9	10
11	12	13	14	15	16	17
18	19	20	21	22	23	24
25	26	27	28	29		

MARCH 2024

S	M	T	W	T	F	S
					1	2
3	4	5	6	7	8	9
10	11	12	13	14	15	16
17	18	19	20	21	22	23
24	25	26	27	28	29	30
31						

Week of February 11–17

"For dust thou art, and into dust thou shalt return."
GENESIS 3:19

WEEKLY GOALS	HABIT TRACKER

                                                                          S M T W T F S

THIS WEEK

MEAL PLAN

Sunday

Monday

Tuesday

Wednesday

Thursday

Friday

Saturday

THINGS TO REMEMBER

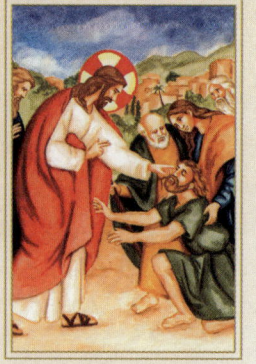

SUNDAY, FEBRUARY 11 / Quinquagesima Sunday

MONDAY, FEBRUARY 12 / Seven Holy Servite Founders

> "Thou shalt sprinkle me with hyssop, and I shall be cleansed: thou shalt wash me, and I shall be made whiter than snow."
>
> PSALMS 50:9

TUESDAY, FEBRUARY 13 / Feria of Septuagesima / Shrove Tuesday

WEDNESDAY, FEBRUARY 14 / Ash Wednesday / Valentine's Day

THURSDAY, FEBRUARY 15 / Feria of Lent

- ☐ ....
- ☐ ....
- ☐ ....
- ☐ ....
- ☐ ....
- ☐ ....
- ☐ ....
- ☐ ....
- ☐ ....
- ☐ ....

FRIDAY, FEBRUARY 16 / Feria of Lent

- ☐ ....
- ☐ ....
- ☐ ....
- ☐ ....
- ☐ ....
- ☐ ....
- ☐ ....
- ☐ ....
- ☐ ....
- ☐ ....

SATURDAY, FEBRUARY 17 / Feria of Lent

- ☐ ....
- ☐ ....
- ☐ ....
- ☐ ....
- ☐ ....
- ☐ ....
- ☐ ....
- ☐ ....
- ☐ ....
- ☐ ....

CALL / EMAIL / FOLLOW-UP

FEBRUARY 2024

S	M	T	W	T	F	S
				1	2	3
4	5	6	7	8	9	10
11	12	13	14	15	16	17
18	19	20	21	22	23	24
25	26	27	28	29		

MARCH 2024

S	M	T	W	T	F	S
					1	2
3	4	5	6	7	8	9
10	11	12	13	14	15	16
17	18	19	20	21	22	23
24	25	26	27	28	29	30
31						

Week of February 18–24

"Devils take great delight in fullness, and drunkenness, and bodily comfort. Fasting possesses great power and it works glorious things. To fast is to banquet with angels."

ST. ATHANASIUS OF ALEXANDRIA

WEEKLY GOALS

HABIT TRACKER

S M T W T F S

THIS WEEK

MEAL PLAN

Sunday

Monday

Tuesday

Wednesday

Thursday

Friday

Saturday

THINGS TO REMEMBER

I **SUNDAY, FEBRUARY 18** / First Sunday of Lent

III **MONDAY, FEBRUARY 19** / Feria of Lent / President's Day

III **TUESDAY, FEBRUARY 20** / Feria of Lent

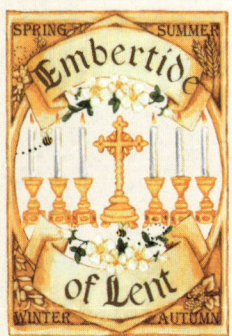

II **WEDNESDAY, FEBRUARY 21** / Ember Wednesday of Lent

THURSDAY, FEBRUARY 22 / Chair of St. Peter

FRIDAY, FEBRUARY 23 / Ember Friday of Lent

SATURDAY, FEBRUARY 24 / St. Matthias

CALL / EMAIL / FOLLOW-UP

FEBRUARY 2024

S	M	T	W	T	F	S
				1	2	3
4	5	6	7	8	9	10
11	12	13	14	15	16	17
18	19	20	21	22	23	24
25	26	27	28	29		

MARCH 2024

S	M	T	W	T	F	S
					1	2
3	4	5	6	7	8	9
10	11	12	13	14	15	16
17	18	19	20	21	22	23
24	25	26	27	28	29	30
31						

March
The Month of St. Joseph

PRAYER FOR MARCH

O St. Joseph, whose protection is so great, so strong, so prompt before the Throne of God, I place in you all my interests and desires. O St. Joseph do assist me by your powerful intercession and obtain for me from your Divine Son all spiritual blessings through Jesus Christ, Our Lord.

—EXCERPT FROM A PRAYER TO ST. JOSEPH THAT WAS FOUND IN A.D. 50

GOALS AND NOTES

March 2024
The Month of St. Joseph

FEBRUARY 2024
S	M	T	W	T	F	S
				1	2	3
4	5	6	7	8	9	10
11	12	13	14	15	16	17
18	19	20	21	22	23	24
25	26	27	28	29		

APRIL 2024
S	M	T	W	T	F	S
	1	2	3	4	5	6
7	8	9	10	11	12	13
14	15	16	17	18	19	20
21	22	23	24	25	26	27
28	29	30				

SUNDAY *Resurrection & Trinity*	MONDAY *Holy Spirit*	TUESDAY *Holy Angels*	WEDNESDAY *St. Joseph*
3 — THIRD SUNDAY OF LENT	**4**	**5**	**6**
10 — Daylight Saving Time Begins — FOURTH SUNDAY OF LENT (LAETARE SUNDAY)	**11**	**12**	**13**
17 — St. Patrick's Day — PASSION SUNDAY	**18**	**19** — ST. JOSEPH, SPOUSE OF THE B.V.M.	**20**
24 — PALM SUNDAY	**25** — FERIA OF HOLY WEEK	**26** — FERIA OF HOLY WEEK	**27** — FERIA OF HOLY WEEK
31 — EASTER SUNDAY			

> "There are many saints to whom God has given the power to assist us in the necessities of life, but the power given to St. Joseph is unlimited: it extends to all our needs, and all those who invoke him with confidence are sure to be heard."
>
> ST. THOMAS AQUINAS

THURSDAY *The Eucharist*	FRIDAY *Christ's Passion*	SATURDAY *The Blessed Virgin Mary*	NOTES
	1	2	
7	8	9	
14	15	16	
21	22	23	
28	29	30	
HOLY THURSDAY	GOOD FRIDAY	HOLY SATURDAY	

Week of February 25–March 2

"I will attempt day by day to break my will into pieces. I want to do God's Holy Will, not my own."
ST. GABRIEL OF OUR LADY OF SORROWS

WEEKLY GOALS

HABIT TRACKER

S M T W T F S

THIS WEEK

MEAL PLAN

Sunday

Monday

Tuesday

Wednesday

Thursday

Friday

Saturday

THINGS TO REMEMBER

I **SUNDAY, FEBRUARY 25** / Second Sunday of Lent

III **MONDAY, FEBRUARY 26** / Feria of Lent

III **TUESDAY, FEBRUARY 27** / Feria of Lent

III **WEDNESDAY, FEBRUARY 28** / Feria of Lent

☰ **THURSDAY, FEBRUARY 29** / Feria of Lent

☐ ....
☐ ....
☐ ....
☐ ....
☐ ....
☐ ....
☐ ....
☐ ....
☐ ....
☐ ....

☰ **FRIDAY, MARCH 1** / Feria of Lent / *First Friday*

☐ ....
☐ ....
☐ ....
☐ ....
☐ ....
☐ ....
☐ ....
☐ ....
☐ ....
☐ ....

☰ **SATURDAY, MARCH 2** / Feria of Lent / *First Saturday*

☐ ....
☐ ....
☐ ....
☐ ....
☐ ....
☐ ....
☐ ....
☐ ....
☐ ....
☐ ....

CALL / EMAIL / FOLLOW-UP

MARCH 2024

S	M	T	W	T	F	S
					1	2
3	4	5	6	7	8	9
10	11	12	13	14	15	16
17	18	19	20	21	22	23
24	25	26	27	28	29	30
31						

APRIL 2024

S	M	T	W	T	F	S
	1	2	3	4	5	6
7	8	9	10	11	12	13
14	15	16	17	18	19	20
21	22	23	24	25	26	27
28	29	30				

Week of March 3–9

"Man cannot live without joy; therefore when he is deprived of true spiritual joys it is necessary that he become addicted to carnal pleasures."
ST. THOMAS AQUINAS

WEEKLY GOALS

HABIT TRACKER

S M T W T F S

THIS WEEK

MEAL PLAN

Sunday

Monday

Tuesday

Wednesday

Thursday

Friday

Saturday

THINGS TO REMEMBER

I **SUNDAY, MARCH 3** / Third Sunday of Lent

III **MONDAY, MARCH 4** / Feria of Lent

III **TUESDAY, MARCH 5** / Feria of Lent

III **WEDNESDAY, MARCH 6** / Feria of Lent

THURSDAY, MARCH 7 / Feria of Lent

FRIDAY, MARCH 8 / Feria of Lent

SATURDAY, MARCH 9 / Feria of Lent

CALL / EMAIL / FOLLOW-UP

MARCH 2024
S	M	T	W	T	F	S
					1	2
3	4	5	6	7	8	9
10	11	12	13	14	15	16
17	18	19	20	21	22	23
24	25	26	27	28	29	30
31						

APRIL 2024
S	M	T	W	T	F	S
	1	2	3	4	5	6
7	8	9	10	11	12	13
14	15	16	17	18	19	20
21	22	23	24	25	26	27
28	29	30				

Week of March 10–16

"He who does not acquire the love of God will scarcely persevere in the grace of God, for it is very difficult to renounce sin merely through fear of chastisement."

ST. ALPHONSUS MARY of LIGUORI

WEEKLY GOALS

HABIT TRACKER

S M T W T F S

THIS WEEK

MEAL PLAN

Sunday

Monday

Tuesday

Wednesday

Thursday

Friday

Saturday

THINGS TO REMEMBER

I **SUNDAY, MARCH 10** / Fourth Sunday of Lent, Laetare Sunday / Daylight Saving Time Begins

III **MONDAY, MARCH 11** / Feria of Lent

III **TUESDAY, MARCH 12** / Feria of Lent

III **WEDNESDAY, MARCH 13** / Feria of Lent

THURSDAY, MARCH 14 / Feria of Lent

FRIDAY, MARCH 15 / Feria of Lent

SATURDAY, MARCH 16 / Feria of Lent

CALL / EMAIL / FOLLOW-UP

MARCH 2024

S	M	T	W	T	F	S
					1	2
3	4	5	6	7	8	9
10	11	12	13	14	15	16
17	18	19	20	21	22	23
24	25	26	27	28	29	30
31						

APRIL 2024

S	M	T	W	T	F	S
	1	2	3	4	5	6
7	8	9	10	11	12	13
14	15	16	17	18	19	20
21	22	23	24	25	26	27
28	29	30				

Week of March 17–23

"Whereas Adam and Eve were the source of evil which was unleashed on the world, Joseph and Mary are the summit from which holiness spreads all over the earth."
POPE JOHN PAUL II

WEEKLY GOALS

HABIT TRACKER

S M T W T F S

THIS WEEK

MEAL PLAN

Sunday

Monday

Tuesday

Wednesday

Thursday

Friday

Saturday

THINGS TO REMEMBER

I **SUNDAY, MARCH 17** / Passion Sunday / St. Patrick's Day

III **MONDAY, MARCH 18** / Feria of Passiontide

I **TUESDAY, MARCH 19** / St. Joseph, Spouse of the B.V.M.

III **WEDNESDAY, MARCH 20** / Feria of Passiontide

THURSDAY, MARCH 21 / Feria of Passiontide

FRIDAY, MARCH 22 / Feria of Passiontide

SATURDAY, MARCH 23 / Feria of Passiontide

CALL / EMAIL / FOLLOW-UP

MARCH 2024

S	M	T	W	T	F	S
					1	2
3	4	5	6	7	8	9
10	11	12	13	14	15	16
17	18	19	20	21	22	23
24	25	26	27	28	29	30
31						

APRIL 2024

S	M	T	W	T	F	S
	1	2	3	4	5	6
7	8	9	10	11	12	13
14	15	16	17	18	19	20
21	22	23	24	25	26	27
28	29	30				

Week of March 24–30

"He who seeks not the Cross of Christ seeks not the glory of Christ."
ST. JOHN OF THE CROSS

WEEKLY GOALS

HABIT TRACKER

S M T W T F S

THIS WEEK

MEAL PLAN

Sunday

Monday

Tuesday

Wednesday

Thursday

Friday

Saturday

THINGS TO REMEMBER

SUNDAY, MARCH 24 / Palm Sunday

MONDAY, MARCH 25 / Feria of Holy Week

TUESDAY, MARCH 26 / Feria of Holy Week

WEDNESDAY, MARCH 27 / Feria of Holy Week

THURSDAY, MARCH 28 / Holy Thursday

☐ ....
☐ ....
☐ ....
☐ ....
☐ ....
☐ ....
☐ ....
☐ ....
☐ ....
☐ ....

FRIDAY, MARCH 29 / Good Friday

☐ ....
☐ ....
☐ ....
☐ ....
☐ ....
☐ ....
☐ ....
☐ ....
☐ ....
☐ ....

SATURDAY, MARCH 30 / Holy Saturday

☐ ....
☐ ....
☐ ....
☐ ....
☐ ....
☐ ....
☐ ....
☐ ....
☐ ....
☐ ....

CALL / EMAIL / FOLLOW-UP

MARCH 2024

S	M	T	W	T	F	S
					1	2
3	4	5	6	7	8	9
10	11	12	13	14	15	16
17	18	19	20	21	22	23
24	25	26	27	28	29	30
31						

APRIL 2024

S	M	T	W	T	F	S
	1	2	3	4	5	6
7	8	9	10	11	12	13
14	15	16	17	18	19	20
21	22	23	24	25	26	27
28	29	30				

April
The Month of the Most Holy Eucharist

PRAYER FOR APRIL

Sweetest Jesus, Body and Blood most Holy, be the delight and pleasure of my soul, my strength and salvation in all temptations, my joy and peace in every trial, my light and guide in every word and deed, and my final protection in death. Amen.

–BY ST. THOMAS AQUINAS, TAKEN FROM *THE AQUINAS PRAYER BOOK*

GOALS AND NOTES

April 2024
The Month of the Most Holy Eucharist

MARCH 2024
S	M	T	W	T	F	S
					1	2
3	4	5	6	7	8	9
10	11	12	13	14	15	16
17	18	19	20	21	22	23
24	25	26	27	28	29	30
31						

MAY 2024
S	M	T	W	T	F	S
			1	2	3	4
5	6	7	8	9	10	11
12	13	14	15	16	17	18
19	20	21	22	23	24	25
26	27	28	29	30	31	

SUNDAY *Resurrection & Trinity*	MONDAY *Holy Spirit*	TUESDAY *Holy Angels*	WEDNESDAY *St. Joseph*
	1 EASTER MONDAY	**2** EASTER TUESDAY	**3** EASTER WEDNESDAY
7 LOW SUNDAY	**8** THE ANNUNCIATION	**9**	**10**
14 Second Sunday after Easter	**15**	**16**	**17**
21 Third Sunday after Easter	**22** Sts. Soter and Cajus	**23**	**24** St. Fidelis of Sigmaringen
21 Fourth Sunday after Easter	**29** St. Peter of Verona	**30** St. Catherine of Siena	

> "To not go to Communion is like someone dying of thirst beside a spring."
> ST. JOHN VIANNEY

THURSDAY *The Eucharist*	FRIDAY *Christ's Passion*	SATURDAY *The Blessed Virgin Mary*
4 EASTER THURSDAY	**5** EASTER FRIDAY	**6** EASTER SATURDAY
11 St. Leo the Great	**12**	**13** St. Hermenegild
18	**19**	**20**
25 **St. Mark the Evangelist Greater Rogations**	**26** Sts. Cletus & Marcellinus	**27** St. Peter Canisius

NOTES

Week of March 31–April 6

"Now all things have been filled with light, both heaven and earth and those beneath the earth; so let all creation sing Christ's rising, by which it is established."

ST. JOHN OF DAMASCUS

WEEKLY GOALS

- [ ]
- [ ]
- [ ]
- [ ]
- [ ]
- [ ]
- [ ]
- [ ]

HABIT TRACKER

	S	M	T	W	T	F	S
___	○	○	○	○	○	○	○
___	○	○	○	○	○	○	○
___	○	○	○	○	○	○	○
___	○	○	○	○	○	○	○
___	○	○	○	○	○	○	○
___	○	○	○	○	○	○	○
___	○	○	○	○	○	○	○
___	○	○	○	○	○	○	○

THIS WEEK

- [ ]
- [ ]
- [ ]
- [ ]
- [ ]
- [ ]
- [ ]
- [ ]
- [ ]
- [ ]
- [ ]
- [ ]
- [ ]
- [ ]
- [ ]
- [ ]
- [ ]
- [ ]
- [ ]
- [ ]

MEAL PLAN

Sunday

Monday

Tuesday

Wednesday

Thursday

Friday

Saturday

THINGS TO REMEMBER

SUNDAY, MARCH 31 / Easter Sunday

MONDAY, APRIL 1 / Easter Monday

TUESDAY, APRIL 2 / Easter Tuesday

WEDNESDAY, APRIL 3 / Easter Wednesday

THURSDAY, APRIL 4 / Easter Thursday

- ....
- ....
- ....
- ....
- ....
- ....
- ....
- ....
- ....
- ....
- ....

FRIDAY, APRIL 5 / Easter Friday / *First Friday*

- ....
- ....
- ....
- ....
- ....
- ....
- ....
- ....
- ....
- ....
- ....

SATURDAY, APRIL 6 / Easter Saturday / *First Saturday*

- ....
- ....
- ....
- ....
- ....
- ....
- ....
- ....
- ....
- ....
- ....

CALL / EMAIL / FOLLOW-UP

APRIL 2024

S	M	T	W	T	F	S
	1	2	3	4	5	6
7	8	9	10	11	12	13
14	15	16	17	18	19	20
21	22	23	24	25	26	27
28	29	30				

MAY 2024

S	M	T	W	T	F	S
			1	2	3	4
5	6	7	8	9	10	11
12	13	14	15	16	17	18
19	20	21	22	23	24	25
26	27	28	29	30	31	

Week of April 7–13

"For I do not seek to understand in order that I may believe, but I believe in order to understand. For this also I believe—that unless I believe I shall not understand."
ST. ANSELM OF CANTERBURY

WEEKLY GOALS

HABIT TRACKER

S M T W T F S

THIS WEEK

MEAL PLAN

Sunday

Monday

Tuesday

Wednesday

Thursday

Friday

Saturday

THINGS TO REMEMBER

[I] **SUNDAY, APRIL 7** / Low Sunday

[I] **MONDAY, APRIL 8** / The Annunciation

> "Behold thou shalt conceive in thy womb, and shalt bring forth a son; and thou shalt call his name Jesus. He shall be great, and shall be called the Son of the most High."
>
> LUKE 1:31-32

[IV] **TUESDAY, APRIL 9** / Feria of Paschaltide

> "Who is he that overcometh the world, but he that believeth that Jesus is the Son of God? This is he that came by water and blood, Jesus Christ."
>
> 1 JOHN 5:5-6

[IV] **WEDNESDAY, APRIL 10** / Feria of Paschaltide

THURSDAY, APRIL 11 / St. Leo the Great

- [ ] ....
- [ ] ....
- [ ] ....
- [ ] ....
- [ ] ....
- [ ] ....
- [ ] ....
- [ ] ....
- [ ] ....
- [ ] ....

FRIDAY, APRIL 12 / Feria of Paschaltide

- [ ] ....
- [ ] ....
- [ ] ....
- [ ] ....
- [ ] ....
- [ ] ....
- [ ] ....
- [ ] ....
- [ ] ....
- [ ] ....

> "Put in thy finger hither, and see my hands; and bring hither thy hand, and put it into my side; and be not faithless, but believing."
>
> **JOHN 20:27**

SATURDAY, APRIL 13 / St. Hermenegild

- [ ] ....
- [ ] ....
- [ ] ....
- [ ] ....
- [ ] ....
- [ ] ....
- [ ] ....
- [ ] ....
- [ ] ....
- [ ] ....

CALL / EMAIL / FOLLOW-UP

APRIL 2024

S	M	T	W	T	F	S
	1	2	3	4	5	6
7	8	9	10	11	12	13
14	15	16	17	18	19	20
21	22	23	24	25	26	27
28	29	30				

MAY 2024

S	M	T	W	T	F	S
			1	2	3	4
5	6	7	8	9	10	11
12	13	14	15	16	17	18
19	20	21	22	23	24	25
26	27	28	29	30	31	

Week of April 14–20

"Entrust yourself entirely to God. He is a Father and a most loving Father at that, who would rather let heaven and earth collapse than abandon anyone who trusted in him."
ST. PAUL OF THE CROSS

WEEKLY GOALS

HABIT TRACKER

S M T W T F S

THIS WEEK

MEAL PLAN

Sunday

Monday

Tuesday

Wednesday

Thursday

Friday

Saturday

THINGS TO REMEMBER

SUNDAY, APRIL 14 / Second Sunday after Easter

"I am the good shepherd. The good shepherd giveth his life for his sheep."
JOHN 10:11

MONDAY, APRIL 15 / Feria of Paschaltide

"For unto this are you called: because Christ also suffered for us, leaving you an example that you should follow his steps."
1 PETER 2:21

TUESDAY, APRIL 16 / Feria of Paschaltide

"Who, when he was reviled, did not revile: when he suffered, he threatened not: but delivered himself to him that judged him unjustly."
1 PETER 2:23

WEDNESDAY, APRIL 17 / Feria of Paschaltide

THURSDAY, APRIL 18 / Feria of Paschaltide

> "Who his own self bore our sins in his body upon the tree: that we, being dead to sins, should live to justice."
> **1 PETER 2:24**

FRIDAY, APRIL 19 / Feria of Paschaltide

> "For you were as sheep going astray; but you are now converted to the shepherd and bishop of your souls."
> **1 PETER 2:25**

SATURDAY, APRIL 20 / Our Lady on Saturday

CALL / EMAIL / FOLLOW-UP

APRIL 2024

S	M	T	W	T	F	S
	1	2	3	4	5	6
7	8	9	10	11	12	13
14	15	16	17	18	19	20
21	22	23	24	25	26	27
28	29	30				

MAY 2024

S	M	T	W	T	F	S
			1	2	3	4
5	6	7	8	9	10	11
12	13	14	15	16	17	18
19	20	21	22	23	24	25
26	27	28	29	30	31	

Week of April 21–27

"Better that only a few Catholics should be left, staunch and sincere in their religion, than that they should, remaining many, desire as it were, to be in collusion with the Church's enemies and in conformity with the open foes of our faith."
ST. PETER CANISIUS

WEEKLY GOALS

HABIT TRACKER

S M T W T F S

THIS WEEK

MEAL PLAN

Sunday

Monday

Tuesday

Wednesday

Thursday

Friday

Saturday

THINGS TO REMEMBER

II **SUNDAY, APRIL 21** / Third Sunday after Easter

III **MONDAY, APRIL 22** / Sts. Soter and Cajus

"For the glory of thy name, O Lord, deliver us: and forgive us our sins for thy name's sake: Lest they should say among the Gentiles: Where is their God?"

PSALMS 78:9-10

IV **TUESDAY, APRIL 23** / Feria of Paschaltide

III **WEDNESDAY, APRIL 24** / St. Fidelis of Sigmaringen

THURSDAY, APRIL 25 / St. Mark the Evangelist / Greater Rogations

FRIDAY, APRIL 26 / Sts. Cletus & Marcellinus

SATURDAY, APRIL 27 / St. Peter Canisius

CALL / EMAIL / FOLLOW-UP

APRIL 2024

S	M	T	W	T	F	S
	1	2	3	4	5	6
7	8	9	10	11	12	13
14	15	16	17	18	19	20
21	22	23	24	25	26	27
28	29	30				

MAY 2024

S	M	T	W	T	F	S
			1	2	3	4
5	6	7	8	9	10	11
12	13	14	15	16	17	18
19	20	21	22	23	24	25
26	27	28	29	30	31	

May
The Month of the Blessed Virgin Mary

PRAYER FOR MAY

Hail, Mary, White Lily of the Glorious and Always-Serene Trinity. Hail, Brilliant Rose of the Garden of Heavenly Delights; O you, by whom God wanted to be born, and by whose milk the King of Heaven wanted to be nourished! Nourish our souls with effusions of divine grace. Amen.

—"HAIL MARY OF GOLD," A PRAYER GIVEN TO ST. GERTRUDE BY OUR LADY

GOALS AND NOTES

May 2024
The Month of the Blessed Virgin Mary

APRIL 2024

S	M	T	W	T	F	S
	1	2	3	4	5	6
7	8	9	10	11	12	13
14	15	16	17	18	19	20
21	22	23	24	25	26	27
28	29	30				

JUNE 2024

S	M	T	W	T	F	S
						1
2	3	4	5	6	7	8
9	10	11	12	13	14	15
16	17	18	19	20	21	22
23	24	25	26	27	28	29
30						

SUNDAY *Resurrection & Trinity*	MONDAY *Holy Spirit*	TUESDAY *Holy Angels*	WEDNESDAY *St. Joseph*
			1 ST. JOSEPH THE WORKMAN
5 Fifth Sunday after Easter	**6** Lesser Rogations	**7** St. Stanislaus Lesser Rogations	**8** Vigil of the Ascension/ Lesser Rogations
12 Mother's Day Sunday after the Ascension	**13** St. Robert Bellarmine	**14**	**15** St. Jean-Baptiste de La Salle
19 PENTECOST SUNDAY	**20** PENTECOST MONDAY	**21** PENTECOST TUESDAY	**22** EMBER WEDNESDAY IN THE OCTAVE OF PENTECOST
26 TRINITY SUNDAY	**27** Memorial Day St. Bede the Venerable	**28** St. Augustine of Canterbury	**29** St. Mary Magdalene of Pazzi

> "Believe me, there is no more powerful means to obtain God's grace than to employ the intercessions of the Holy Virgin."
>
> ST. PHILIP NERI

THURSDAY *The Eucharist*	FRIDAY *Christ's Passion*	SATURDAY *The Blessed Virgin Mary*	NOTES
2 St. Athanasius of Alexandria	**3**	**4** St. Monica	
9 THE ASCENSION OF OUR LORD *Holy Day of Obligation*	**10** St. Antoninus of Florence	**11** Sts. Philip and James	
16 St. Ubald	**17** St. Paschal Baylon	**18** VIGIL OF PENTECOST	
23 PENTECOST THURSDAY	**24** EMBER FRIDAY IN THE OCTAVE OF PENTECOST	**25** EMBER SATURDAY IN THE OCTAVE OF PENTECOST	
30 CORPUS CHRISTI	**31** Queenship of Mary		

Week of April 28–May 4

"Carefully study to present thyself approved unto God, a workman that needeth not to be ashamed, rightly handling the word of truth."

2 TIMOTHY 2:15

WEEKLY GOALS

HABIT TRACKER

S M T W T F S

THIS WEEK

MEAL PLAN

Sunday

Monday

Tuesday

Wednesday

Thursday

Friday

Saturday

THINGS TO REMEMBER

SUNDAY, APRIL 28 / Fourth Sunday after Easter

MONDAY, APRIL 29 / St. Peter of Verona

TUESDAY, APRIL 30 / St. Catherine of Siena

WEDNESDAY, MAY 1 / St. Joseph the Workman

THURSDAY, MAY 2 / St. Athanasius of Alexandria

- [ ] ....
- [ ] ....
- [ ] ....
- [ ] ....
- [ ] ....
- [ ] ....
- [ ] ....
- [ ] ....
- [ ] ....
- [ ] ....

FRIDAY, MAY 3 / Feria of Paschaltide / *First Friday*

- [ ] ....
- [ ] ....
- [ ] ....
- [ ] ....
- [ ] ....
- [ ] ....
- [ ] ....
- [ ] ....
- [ ] ....
- [ ] ....

> "Let the brightness of the Lord our God be upon us: and direct thou the works of our hands."
>
> **PSALMS 89:17**

SATURDAY, MAY 4 / St. Monica / *First Saturday*

- [ ] ....
- [ ] ....
- [ ] ....
- [ ] ....
- [ ] ....
- [ ] ....
- [ ] ....
- [ ] ....
- [ ] ....
- [ ] ....

CALL / EMAIL / FOLLOW-UP

MAY 2024

S	M	T	W	T	F	S
			1	2	3	4
5	6	7	8	9	10	11
12	13	14	15	16	17	18
19	20	21	22	23	24	25
26	27	28	29	30	31	

JUNE 2024

S	M	T	W	T	F	S
						1
2	3	4	5	6	7	8
9	10	11	12	13	14	15
16	17	18	19	20	21	22
23	24	25	26	27	28	29
30						

Week of May 5–11

"You ascended before our eyes, and we turned back grieving, only to find You in our hearts."
ST. AUGUSTINE

WEEKLY GOALS

HABIT TRACKER

S M T W T F S

THIS WEEK

MEAL PLAN

Sunday

Monday

Tuesday

Wednesday

Thursday

Friday

Saturday

THINGS TO REMEMBER

SUNDAY, MAY 5 / Fifth Sunday after Easter

MONDAY, MAY 6 / Lesser Rogations

TUESDAY, MAY 7 / Lesser Rogations / St. Stanislaus

WEDNESDAY, MAY 8 / Vigil of the Ascension / Lesser Rogations

THURSDAY, MAY 9 / The Ascension of Our Lord / *Holy Day of Obligation*

FRIDAY, MAY 10 / St. Antoninus of Florence

SATURDAY, MAY 11 / Sts. Philip and James

CALL / EMAIL / FOLLOW-UP

MAY 2024

S	M	T	W	T	F	S
			1	2	3	4
5	6	7	8	9	10	11
12	13	14	15	16	17	18
19	20	21	22	23	24	25
26	27	28	29	30	31	

JUNE 2024

S	M	T	W	T	F	S
						1
2	3	4	5	6	7	8
9	10	11	12	13	14	15
16	17	18	19	20	21	22
23	24	25	26	27	28	29
30						

Week of May 12–18

"But you shall receive the power of the Holy Ghost coming upon you, and you shall be witnesses unto me in Jerusalem, and in all Judea, and Samaria, and even to the uttermost part of the earth."

ACTS 1:8

WEEKLY GOALS

HABIT TRACKER

S M T W T F S

THIS WEEK

MEAL PLAN

Sunday

Monday

Tuesday

Wednesday

Thursday

Friday

Saturday

THINGS TO REMEMBER

SUNDAY, MAY 12 / Sunday after the Ascension / Mother's Day

MONDAY, MAY 13 / St. Robert Bellarmine

"But when the Paraclete cometh, whom I will send you from the Father, the Spirit of truth,… he shall give testimony of me."

JOHN 15:26

TUESDAY, MAY 14 / Feria of Paschaltide

WEDNESDAY, MAY 15 / St. Jean-Baptiste de La Salle

THURSDAY, MAY 16 / St. Ubald

- [ ] ....
- [ ] ....
- [ ] ....
- [ ] ....
- [ ] ....
- [ ] ....
- [ ] ....
- [ ] ....
- [ ] ....
- [ ] ....

FRIDAY, MAY 17 / St. Paschal Baylon

- [ ] ....
- [ ] ....
- [ ] ....
- [ ] ....
- [ ] ....
- [ ] ....
- [ ] ....
- [ ] ....
- [ ] ....
- [ ] ....

SATURDAY, MAY 18 / Vigil of Pentecost

- [ ] ....
- [ ] ....
- [ ] ....
- [ ] ....
- [ ] ....
- [ ] ....
- [ ] ....
- [ ] ....
- [ ] ....
- [ ] ....

CALL / EMAIL / FOLLOW-UP

MAY 2024

S	M	T	W	T	F	S
			1	2	3	4
5	6	7	8	9	10	11
12	13	14	15	16	17	18
19	20	21	22	23	24	25
26	27	28	29	30	31	

JUNE 2024

S	M	T	W	T	F	S
						1
2	3	4	5	6	7	8
9	10	11	12	13	14	15
16	17	18	19	20	21	22
23	24	25	26	27	28	29
30						

Week of May 19–25

"O Holy Spirit, descend plentifully into my heart. Enlighten the dark corners of this neglected dwelling and scatter there Thy cheerful beams."

ST. AUGUSTINE

WEEKLY GOALS

- [ ]
- [ ]
- [ ]
- [ ]
- [ ]
- [ ]
- [ ]
- [ ]
- [ ]

HABIT TRACKER

	S	M	T	W	T	F	S
___	○	○	○	○	○	○	○
___	○	○	○	○	○	○	○
___	○	○	○	○	○	○	○
___	○	○	○	○	○	○	○
___	○	○	○	○	○	○	○
___	○	○	○	○	○	○	○
___	○	○	○	○	○	○	○
___	○	○	○	○	○	○	○

THIS WEEK

- [ ]
- [ ]
- [ ]
- [ ]
- [ ]
- [ ]
- [ ]
- [ ]
- [ ]
- [ ]
- [ ]
- [ ]
- [ ]
- [ ]
- [ ]
- [ ]
- [ ]
- [ ]
- [ ]
- [ ]

MEAL PLAN

Sunday

Monday

Tuesday

Wednesday

Thursday

Friday

Saturday

THINGS TO REMEMBER

SUNDAY, MAY 19 / Pentecost Sunday

MONDAY, MAY 20 / Pentecost Monday

TUESDAY, MAY 21 / Pentecost Tuesday

WEDNESDAY, MAY 22 / Ember Wednesday in the Octave of Pentecost

THURSDAY, MAY 23 / Pentecost Thursday

☐ ....
☐ ....
☐ ....
☐ ....
☐ ....
☐ ....
☐ ....
☐ ....
☐ ....
☐ ....

FRIDAY, MAY 24 / Ember Friday in the Octave of Pentecost

☐ ....
☐ ....
☐ ....
☐ ....
☐ ....
☐ ....
☐ ....
☐ ....
☐ ....
☐ ....

SATURDAY, MAY 25 / Ember Saturday in the Octave of Pentecost

☐ ....
☐ ....
☐ ....
☐ ....
☐ ....
☐ ....
☐ ....
☐ ....
☐ ....
☐ ....

CALL / EMAIL / FOLLOW-UP

MAY 2024

S	M	T	W	T	F	S
			1	2	3	4
5	6	7	8	9	10	11
12	13	14	15	16	17	18
19	20	21	22	23	24	25
26	27	28	29	30	31	

JUNE 2024

S	M	T	W	T	F	S
						1
2	3	4	5	6	7	8
9	10	11	12	13	14	15
16	17	18	19	20	21	22
23	24	25	26	27	28	29
30						

June

The Month of the Sacred Heart

PRAYER FOR JUNE

O most Sacred Heart of Jesus, pour down Thy blessings abundantly upon Thy Church, upon the Supreme Pontiff, and upon all the clergy; give perseverance to the just, convert sinners, enlighten unbelievers, bless our parents, friends and benefactors, help the dying, free the souls from Purgatory, and extend over all hearts the sweet empire of Thy love. Amen.

–PRE-1968 INDULGENCE OF 500 DAYS

GOALS AND NOTES

June 2024
The Month of the Sacred Heart

MAY 2024
S	M	T	W	T	F	S
			1	2	3	4
5	6	7	8	9	10	11
12	13	14	15	16	17	18
19	20	21	22	23	24	25
26	27	28	29	30	31	

JULY 2024
S	M	T	W	T	F	S
	1	2	3	4	5	6
7	8	9	10	11	12	13
14	15	16	17	18	19	20
21	22	23	24	25	26	27
28	29	30	31			

SUNDAY *Resurrection & Trinity*	MONDAY *Holy Spirit*	TUESDAY *Holy Angels*	WEDNESDAY *St. Joseph*
2 Second Sunday after Pentecost	**3**	**4** St. Francis Caracciolo	**5** St. Boniface
9 Third Sunday after Pentecost	**10** St. Margaret of Scotland	**11** St. Barnabas the Apostle	**12** St. John of San Facundo
16 Father's Day — Fourth Sunday after Pentecost	**17** St. Gregory Barbarigo	**18** St. Ephrem of Syria	**19** St. Juliana Falconieri
23 Fifth Sunday after Pentecost	**24** NATIVITY OF ST. JOHN THE BAPTIST	**25** St. William of Montevergine	**26** Sts. John and Paul
30 Sixth Sunday after Pentecost			

> "O Sacred Heart of Jesus, fountain of eternal life, Your Heart is a glowing furnace of Love. You are my refuge and my sanctuary."
>
> ST. GERTRUDE

THURSDAY *The Eucharist*	FRIDAY *Christ's Passion*	SATURDAY *The Blessed Virgin Mary*
		1 St. Angela Merici
6 St. Norbert of Xanten	7 **SACRED HEART OF JESUS**	8
13 St. Anthony of Padua	14 St. Basil the Great	15
20	21 St. Aloysius Gonzaga	22 St. Paulinus of Nola
27	28 Vigil of Sts. Peter and Paul	29 **STS. PETER AND PAUL**

NOTES

Week of May 26–June 1

"The devotion to the Eucharist is the most noble because it has God as its object; it is the most profitable for salvation, because It gives us the Author of Grace; it is the sweetest, because the Lord is Sweetness Itself."
ST. PIUS X

WEEKLY GOALS

HABIT TRACKER

S M T W T F S

THIS WEEK

MEAL PLAN

Sunday

Monday

Tuesday

Wednesday

Thursday

Friday

Saturday

THINGS TO REMEMBER

SUNDAY, MAY 26 / Trinity Sunday

MONDAY, MAY 27 / St. Bede the Venerable / Memorial Day

TUESDAY, MAY 28 / St. Augustine of Canterbury

WEDNESDAY, MAY 29 / St. Mary Magdalene of Pazzi

THURSDAY, MAY 30 / Corpus Christi

FRIDAY, MAY 31 / Queenship of Mary

SATURDAY, JUNE 1 / St. Angela Merici / *First Saturday*

CALL / EMAIL / FOLLOW-UP

JUNE 2024

S	M	T	W	T	F	S
						1
2	3	4	5	6	7	8
9	10	11	12	13	14	15
16	17	18	19	20	21	22
23	24	25	26	27	28	29
30						

JULY 2024

S	M	T	W	T	F	S
	1	2	3	4	5	6
7	8	9	10	11	12	13
14	15	16	17	18	19	20
21	22	23	24	25	26	27
28	29	30	31			

Week of June 2–8

"O Sacred Heart of Jesus, fountain of eternal life, Your Heart is a glowing furnace of Love. You are my refuge and my sanctuary."

ST. GERTRUDE THE GREAT

WEEKLY GOALS

HABIT TRACKER

S M T W T F S

THIS WEEK

MEAL PLAN

Sunday

Monday

Tuesday

Wednesday

Thursday

Friday

Saturday

THINGS TO REMEMBER

SUNDAY, JUNE 2 / Second Sunday after Pentecost

> "The counsel of the Lord standeth for ever: the thoughts of his heart to all generations.... To deliver their souls from death; and feed them in famine."
>
> **PSALMS 32:11,19**

MONDAY, JUNE 3 / Feria

TUESDAY, JUNE 4 / St. Francis Caracciolo

WEDNESDAY, JUNE 5 / St. Boniface

THURSDAY, JUNE 6 / St. Norbert of Xanten

FRIDAY, JUNE 7 / Sacred Heart of Jesus / *First Friday*

SATURDAY, JUNE 8 / Our Lady on Saturday

CALL / EMAIL / FOLLOW-UP

JUNE 2024

S	M	T	W	T	F	S
						1
2	3	4	5	6	7	8
9	10	11	12	13	14	15
16	17	18	19	20	21	22
23	24	25	26	27	28	29
30						

JULY 2024

S	M	T	W	T	F	S
	1	2	3	4	5	6
7	8	9	10	11	12	13
14	15	16	17	18	19	20
21	22	23	24	25	26	27
28	29	30	31			

Week of June 9–15

"Love of God is not something that can be taught. We did not learn from someone else how to rejoice in light or want to live, or to love our parents or guardians. It is the same—perhaps even more so—with our love for God: it does not come by another's teaching."

ST. BASIL THE GREAT

WEEKLY GOALS

HABIT TRACKER

S M T W T F S

THIS WEEK

MEAL PLAN

Sunday

Monday

Tuesday

Wednesday

Thursday

Friday

Saturday

THINGS TO REMEMBER

▊ **SUNDAY, JUNE 9** / Third Sunday after Pentecost

▊▊ **MONDAY, JUNE 10** / St. Margaret of Scotland

▊▊▊ **TUESDAY, JUNE 11** / St. Barnabas the Apostle

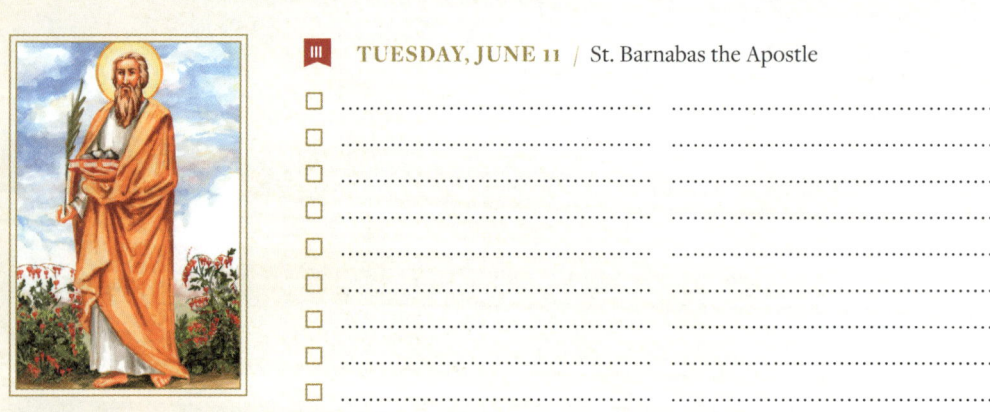

▊▊▊ **WEDNESDAY, JUNE 12** / St. John of San Facundo

THURSDAY, JUNE 13 / St. Anthony of Padua

- [ ] ....
- [ ] ....
- [ ] ....
- [ ] ....
- [ ] ....
- [ ] ....
- [ ] ....
- [ ] ....
- [ ] ....
- [ ] ....

FRIDAY, JUNE 14 / St. Basil the Great

- [ ] ....
- [ ] ....
- [ ] ....
- [ ] ....
- [ ] ....
- [ ] ....
- [ ] ....
- [ ] ....
- [ ] ....
- [ ] ....

SATURDAY, JUNE 15 / Our Lady on Saturday

- [ ] ....
- [ ] ....
- [ ] ....
- [ ] ....
- [ ] ....
- [ ] ....
- [ ] ....
- [ ] ....
- [ ] ....
- [ ] ....

CALL / EMAIL / FOLLOW-UP

JUNE 2024

S	M	T	W	T	F	S
						1
2	3	4	5	6	7	8
9	10	11	12	13	14	15
16	17	18	19	20	21	22
23	24	25	26	27	28	29
30						

JULY 2024

S	M	T	W	T	F	S
	1	2	3	4	5	6
7	8	9	10	11	12	13
14	15	16	17	18	19	20
21	22	23	24	25	26	27
28	29	30	31			

Week of June 16–22

"It is better to be the child of God than king of the whole world."
ST. ALOYSIUS GONZAGA

WEEKLY GOALS

HABIT TRACKER

S M T W T F S

THIS WEEK

MEAL PLAN

Sunday

Monday

Tuesday

Wednesday

Thursday

Friday

Saturday

THINGS TO REMEMBER

SUNDAY, JUNE 16 / Fourth Sunday after Pentecost / Father's Day

MONDAY, JUNE 17 / St. Gregory Barbarigo

TUESDAY, JUNE 18 / St. Ephrem of Syria

WEDNESDAY, JUNE 19 / St. Juliana Falconieri

THURSDAY, JUNE 20 / Feria

FRIDAY, JUNE 21 / St. Aloysius Gonzaga

SATURDAY, JUNE 22 / St. Paulinus of Nola

"The Lord is my firmament, my refuge, and my deliverer. My God is my helper, and in him will I put my trust."

PSALMS 17:3

CALL / EMAIL / FOLLOW-UP

JUNE 2024

S	M	T	W	T	F	S
						1
2	3	4	5	6	7	8
9	10	11	12	13	14	15
16	17	18	19	20	21	22
23	24	25	26	27	28	29
30						

JULY 2024

S	M	T	W	T	F	S
	1	2	3	4	5	6
7	8	9	10	11	12	13
14	15	16	17	18	19	20
21	22	23	24	25	26	27
28	29	30	31			

Week of June 23–29

"What really matters in life is that we are loved by Christ and that we love Him in return."
POPE JOHN PAUL II

WEEKLY GOALS

HABIT TRACKER

S M T W T F S

THIS WEEK

MEAL PLAN

Sunday

Monday

Tuesday

Wednesday

Thursday

Friday

Saturday

THINGS TO REMEMBER

SUNDAY, JUNE 23 / Fifth Sunday after Pentecost

MONDAY, JUNE 24 / Nativity of St. John the Baptist

TUESDAY, JUNE 25 / St. William of Montevergine

WEDNESDAY, JUNE 26 / Sts. John and Paul

IV **THURSDAY, JUNE 27** / Feria

> "But I say to you, that whosoever is angry with his brother, shall be in danger of the judgment."
>
> **MATTHEW 5:22**

II **FRIDAY, JUNE 28** / Vigil of Sts. Peter and Paul

I **SATURDAY, JUNE 29** / Sts. Peter and Paul

CALL / EMAIL / FOLLOW-UP

JUNE 2024

S	M	T	W	T	F	S
						1
2	3	4	5	6	7	8
9	10	11	12	13	14	15
16	17	18	19	20	21	22
23	24	25	26	27	28	29
30						

JULY 2024

S	M	T	W	T	F	S
	1	2	3	4	5	6
7	8	9	10	11	12	13
14	15	16	17	18	19	20
21	22	23	24	25	26	27
28	29	30	31			

July

The Month of the Most Precious Blood

PRAYER FOR JULY

Precious Blood, ocean of divine mercy: Flow upon us! Precious Blood, most pure offering: Procure us every grace! Precious Blood, hope and refuge of sinners: Atone for us! Precious Blood, delight of holy souls: Draw us! Amen.

—THE "CONSTANT" PRAYER OF ST. CATHERINE OF SIENA

GOALS AND NOTES

July 2024
The Month of the Most Precious Blood

JUNE 2024

S	M	T	W	T	F	S
						1
2	3	4	5	6	7	8
9	10	11	12	13	14	15
16	17	18	19	20	21	22
23	24	25	26	27	28	29
30						

AUGUST 2024

S	M	T	W	T	F	S
				1	2	3
4	5	6	7	8	9	10
11	12	13	14	15	16	17
18	19	20	21	22	23	24
25	26	27	28	29	30	31

SUNDAY *Resurrection & Trinity*	MONDAY *Holy Spirit*	TUESDAY *Holy Angels*	WEDNESDAY *St. Joseph*
	1 THE MOST PRECIOUS BLOOD	**2** The Visitation of Our Lady	**3** St. Irenaeus of Lyons
7 Seventh Sunday after Pentecost	**8** St. Elizabeth of Portugal	**9**	**10** The Seven Holy Brothers
14 Eighth Sunday after Pentecost	**15** St. Henry II	**16**	**17**
21 Ninth Sunday after Pentecost	**22** St. Mary Magdalene	**23** St. Apollinaris	**24**
28 Tenth Sunday after Pentecost	**29** St. Martha	**30**	**31** St. Ignatius of Loyola

> "Almighty Father, I place the Precious Blood of Jesus before my lips before I pray, that my prayers may be purified before they ascend to Your divine altar."
>
> ST. MARY MAGDALEN DE PAZZI

THURSDAY *The Eucharist*	FRIDAY *Christ's Passion*	SATURDAY *The Blessed Virgin Mary*
4 Independence Day	**5** St. Anthony Mary Zaccaria	**6**
11	**12** St. John Gualbert	**13**
18 St. Camillus de Lellis	**19** St. Vincent de Paul	**20** St. Jerome Emiliani
25 St. James the Great	**26** St. Anne, Mother of the B.V.M.	**27**

NOTES

Week of June 30–July 6

"Don't hold yourselves cheap, seeing that the Creator of all things and of you estimates your value so high, so dear, that He pours out for you every day the Most Precious Blood of His only-begotten Son."
ST. AUGUSTINE

WEEKLY GOALS

HABIT TRACKER

S M T W T F S

THIS WEEK

MEAL PLAN

Sunday

Monday

Tuesday

Wednesday

Thursday

Friday

Saturday

THINGS TO REMEMBER

SUNDAY, JUNE 30 / Sixth Sunday after Pentecost

MONDAY, JULY 1 / The Most Precious Blood

TUESDAY, JULY 2 / The Visitation of Our Lady

WEDNESDAY, JULY 3 / St. Irenaeus of Lyons

IV **THURSDAY, JULY 4** / Feria / Independence Day

- ....
- ....
- ....
- ....
- ....
- ....
- ....
- ....
- ....
- ....

> "I have gone round, and have offered up in his tabernacle a sacrifice of jubilation: I will sing, and recite a psalm to the Lord."
>
> **PSALMS 26:6**

III **FRIDAY, JULY 5** / St. Anthony Mary Zaccaria / *First Friday*

- ....
- ....
- ....
- ....
- ....
- ....
- ....
- ....
- ....
- ....

IV **SATURDAY, JULY 6** / Our Lady on Saturday / *First Saturday*

- ....
- ....
- ....
- ....
- ....
- ....
- ....
- ....
- ....
- ....

CALL / EMAIL / FOLLOW-UP

JULY 2024

S	M	T	W	T	F	S
	1	2	3	4	5	6
7	8	9	10	11	12	13
14	15	16	17	18	19	20
21	22	23	24	25	26	27
28	29	30	31			

AUGUST 2024

S	M	T	W	T	F	S
				1	2	3
4	5	6	7	8	9	10
11	12	13	14	15	16	17
18	19	20	21	22	23	24
25	26	27	28	29	30	31

Week of July 7–13

"A tree is known by its fruit; a man by his deeds. A good deed is never lost; he who sows courtesy reaps friendship, and he who plants kindness gathers love."

ST. BASIL THE GREAT

WEEKLY GOALS

HABIT TRACKER

S M T W T F S

THIS WEEK

MEAL PLAN

Sunday

Monday

Tuesday

Wednesday

Thursday

Friday

Saturday

THINGS TO REMEMBER

II   SUNDAY, JULY 7 / Seventh Sunday after Pentecost

III   MONDAY, JULY 8 / St. Elizabeth of Portugal

"A good tree cannot bring forth evil fruit, neither can an evil tree bring forth good fruit."

MATTHEW 7:18

IV   TUESDAY, JULY 9 / Feria

III   WEDNESDAY, JULY 10 / The Seven Holy Brothers

IV **THURSDAY, JULY 11** / Feria

☐ ....
☐ ....
☐ ....
☐ ....
☐ ....
☐ ....
☐ ....
☐ ....
☐ ....
☐ ....

III **FRIDAY, JULY 12** / St. John Gualbert

☐ ....
☐ ....
☐ ....
☐ ....
☐ ....
☐ ....
☐ ....
☐ ....
☐ ....
☐ ....

IV **SATURDAY, JULY 13** / Our Lady on Saturday

☐ ....
☐ ....
☐ ....
☐ ....
☐ ....
☐ ....
☐ ....
☐ ....
☐ ....
☐ ....

CALL / EMAIL / FOLLOW-UP

> "Not every one that saith to me, Lord, Lord, shall enter into the kingdom of heaven: but he that doth the will of my Father."
>
> **MATTHEW 7:21**

JULY 2024

S	M	T	W	T	F	S
	1	2	3	4	5	6
7	8	9	10	11	12	13
14	15	16	17	18	19	20
21	22	23	24	25	26	27
28	29	30	31			

AUGUST 2024

S	M	T	W	T	F	S
				1	2	3
4	5	6	7	8	9	10
11	12	13	14	15	16	17
18	19	20	21	22	23	24
25	26	27	28	29	30	31

Week of July 14–20

"Friendships begun in this world will be taken up again, never to be broken off."
ST. FRANCIS DE SALES

WEEKLY GOALS

HABIT TRACKER

S M T W T F S

THIS WEEK

MEAL PLAN

Sunday

Monday

Tuesday

Wednesday

Thursday

Friday

Saturday

THINGS TO REMEMBER

SUNDAY, JULY 14 / Eighth Sunday after Pentecost

MONDAY, JULY 15 / St. Henry II

"Make unto you friends of the mammon of iniquity; that when you shall fail, they may receive you into everlasting dwellings."
LUKE 16:9

TUESDAY, JULY 16 / Feria

"He that is faithful in that which is least, is faithful also in that which is greater."
LUKE 16:10

WEDNESDAY, JULY 17 / Feria

THURSDAY, JULY 18 / St. Camillus de Lellis

FRIDAY, JULY 19 / St. Vincent de Paul

SATURDAY, JULY 20 / St. Jerome Emiliani

CALL / EMAIL / FOLLOW-UP

JULY 2024

S	M	T	W	T	F	S
	1	2	3	4	5	6
7	8	9	10	11	12	13
14	15	16	17	18	19	20
21	22	23	24	25	26	27
28	29	30	31			

AUGUST 2024

S	M	T	W	T	F	S
				1	2	3
4	5	6	7	8	9	10
11	12	13	14	15	16	17
18	19	20	21	22	23	24
25	26	27	28	29	30	31

Week of July 21–27

"The loveliest masterpiece of the heart of God is the heart of a mother."
ST. THÉRÈSE OF LISIEUX

WEEKLY GOALS

- [ ]
- [ ]
- [ ]
- [ ]
- [ ]
- [ ]
- [ ]
- [ ]
- [ ]

HABIT TRACKER

	S	M	T	W	T	F	S
___	○	○	○	○	○	○	○
___	○	○	○	○	○	○	○
___	○	○	○	○	○	○	○
___	○	○	○	○	○	○	○
___	○	○	○	○	○	○	○
___	○	○	○	○	○	○	○
___	○	○	○	○	○	○	○
___	○	○	○	○	○	○	○

THIS WEEK

- [ ]
- [ ]
- [ ]
- [ ]
- [ ]
- [ ]
- [ ]
- [ ]
- [ ]
- [ ]
- [ ]
- [ ]
- [ ]
- [ ]
- [ ]
- [ ]
- [ ]
- [ ]
- [ ]
- [ ]

MEAL PLAN

Sunday

Monday

Tuesday

Wednesday

Thursday

Friday

Saturday

THINGS TO REMEMBER

II SUNDAY, JULY 21 / Ninth Sunday after Pentecost

III MONDAY, JULY 22 / St. Mary Magdalene

III TUESDAY, JULY 23 / St. Apollinaris

"For the days shall come upon thee, and thy enemies shall cast a trench about thee, and compass thee round, and straiten thee on every side."

LUKE 19:43

IV WEDNESDAY, JULY 24 / Feria

THURSDAY, JULY 25 / St. James the Great

FRIDAY, JULY 26 / St. Anne, Mother of the B.V.M.

SATURDAY, JULY 27 / Our Lady on Saturday

CALL / EMAIL / FOLLOW-UP

JULY 2024

S	M	T	W	T	F	S
	1	2	3	4	5	6
7	8	9	10	11	12	13
14	15	16	17	18	19	20
21	22	23	24	25	26	27
28	29	30	31			

AUGUST 2024

S	M	T	W	T	F	S
				1	2	3
4	5	6	7	8	9	10
11	12	13	14	15	16	17
18	19	20	21	22	23	24
25	26	27	28	29	30	31

August
The Month of the Immaculate Heart

PRAYER FOR AUGUST

Almighty everlasting God, who in the heart of the blessed Virgin Mary didst prepare a dwelling worthy of the Holy Ghost; grant in Thy mercy, that we who with devout minds celebrate the festival of that immaculate heart, may be able to live according to Thine own Heart.

—COLLECT FROM THE MASS OF THE IMMACULATE HEART

GOALS AND NOTES

August 2024
The Month of the Immaculate Heart

JULY 2024
S	M	T	W	T	F	S
	1	2	3	4	5	6
7	8	9	10	11	12	13
14	15	16	17	18	19	20
21	22	23	24	25	26	27
28	29	30	31			

SEPTEMBER 2024
S	M	T	W	T	F	S
1	2	3	4	5	6	7
8	9	10	11	12	13	14
15	16	17	18	19	20	21
22	23	24	25	26	27	28
29	30					

SUNDAY *Resurrection & Trinity*	MONDAY *Holy Spirit*	TUESDAY *Holy Angels*	WEDNESDAY *St. Joseph*
4 — Eleventh Sunday after Pentecost	**5** — The Dedication of Our Lady of the Snows	**6** — The Transfiguration	**7** — St. Cajetan
11 — Twelfth Sunday after Pentecost	**12** — St. Clare of Assisi	**13**	**14** — Vigil of the Assumption
18 — Thirteenth Sunday after Pentecost	**19** — St. John Eudes	**20** — St. Bernard of Clairvaux	**21** — St. Jane Frances de Chantal
25 — Fourteenth Sunday after Pentecost	**26**	**27** — St. Joseph Calasance	**28** — St. Augustine

> "Tell everybody that God grants graces through the Immaculate Heart of Mary."
>
> ST. JACINTA

THURSDAY *The Eucharist*	FRIDAY *Christ's Passion*	SATURDAY *The Blessed Virgin Mary*
1	**2** St. Alphonsus Mary of Liguori	**3**
8 St. John Mary Vianney	**9** Vigil of St. Lawrence	**10** St. Lawrence
15 THE ASSUMPTION OF OUR LADY *Holy Day of Obligation*	**16** St. Joachim, Father of the B.V.M.	**17** St. Hyacinth
22 Immaculate Heart of the B.V.M.	**23** St. Philip Benizi	**24** St. Bartholomew the Apostle
29 The Beheading of St. John the Baptist	**30** St. Rose of Lima	**31** St. Raymond Nonnatus

NOTES

Week of July 28–August 3

"Remember: The sinner who is sorry for his sins is closer to God than the just man who boasts of his good works."
ST. PADRE PIO

WEEKLY GOALS

HABIT TRACKER

S M T W T F S

THIS WEEK

MEAL PLAN

Sunday

Monday

Tuesday

Wednesday

Thursday

Friday

Saturday

THINGS TO REMEMBER

II **SUNDAY, JULY 28** / Tenth Sunday after Pentecost

IIII **MONDAY, JULY 29** / St. Martha

"Every one that exalteth himself, shall be humbled: and he that humbleth himself, shall be exalted."

LUKE 18:14

IV **TUESDAY, JULY 30** / Feria

III **WEDNESDAY, JULY 31** / St. Ignatius of Loyola

IV **THURSDAY, AUGUST 1** / Feria

> "To thee, O Lord, have I lifted up my soul. In thee, O my God, I put my trust; let me not be ashamed."
>
> PSALMS 24:1–2

III **FRIDAY, AUGUST 2** / St. Alphonsus Mary of Liguori / *First Friday*

IV **SATURDAY, AUGUST 3** / Our Lady on Saturday / *First Saturday*

CALL / EMAIL / FOLLOW-UP

AUGUST 2024

S	M	T	W	T	F	S
				1	2	3
4	5	6	7	8	9	10
11	12	13	14	15	16	17
18	19	20	21	22	23	24
25	26	27	28	29	30	31

SEPTEMBER 2024

S	M	T	W	T	F	S
1	2	3	4	5	6	7
8	9	10	11	12	13	14
15	16	17	18	19	20	21
22	23	24	25	26	27	28
29	30					

Week of August 4–10

"Place your mind before the mirror of eternity! Place your soul in the brilliance of glory! And transform your entire being into the image of the Godhead Itself through contemplation."

ST. CLARE OF ASSISI

WEEKLY GOALS

HABIT TRACKER

S M T W T F S

THIS WEEK

MEAL PLAN

Sunday

Monday

Tuesday

Wednesday

Thursday

Friday

Saturday

THINGS TO REMEMBER

SUNDAY, AUGUST 4 / Eleventh Sunday after Pentecost

MONDAY, AUGUST 5 / The Dedication of Our Lady of the Snows

TUESDAY, AUGUST 6 / The Transfiguration

WEDNESDAY, AUGUST 7 / St. Cajetan

THURSDAY, AUGUST 8 / St. John Mary Vianney

FRIDAY, AUGUST 9 / Vigil of St. Lawrence

SATURDAY, AUGUST 10 / St. Lawrence

CALL / EMAIL / FOLLOW-UP

AUGUST 2024
S	M	T	W	T	F	S
				1	2	3
4	5	6	7	8	9	10
11	12	13	14	15	16	17
18	19	20	21	22	23	24
25	26	27	28	29	30	31

SEPTEMBER 2024
S	M	T	W	T	F	S
1	2	3	4	5	6	7
8	9	10	11	12	13	14
15	16	17	18	19	20	21
22	23	24	25	26	27	28
29	30					

Week of August 11–17

"Jesus honored her before all ages and will honor her for all ages. No one comes to Him, nor even near Him, no one is saved or sanctified, if he too will not honor her. This is the lot of angels and of men."

ST. MAXIMILIAN KOLBE

WEEKLY GOALS

HABIT TRACKER

S M T W T F S

THIS WEEK

MEAL PLAN

Sunday

Monday

Tuesday

Wednesday

Thursday

Friday

Saturday

THINGS TO REMEMBER

SUNDAY, AUGUST 11 / Twelfth Sunday after Pentecost

MONDAY, AUGUST 12 / St. Clare of Assisi

"Sing ye to the Lord a new canticle: because he hath done wonderful things."

PSALMS 97:1

TUESDAY, AUGUST 13 / Feria

WEDNESDAY, AUGUST 14 / Vigil of the Assumption

THURSDAY, AUGUST 15 / The Assumption of Our Lady / *Holy Day of Obligation*

FRIDAY, AUGUST 16 / St. Joachim, Father of the B.V.M.

SATURDAY, AUGUST 17 / St. Hyacinth

CALL / EMAIL / FOLLOW-UP

AUGUST 2024

S	M	T	W	T	F	S
				1	2	3
4	5	6	7	8	9	10
11	12	13	14	15	16	17
18	19	20	21	22	23	24
25	26	27	28	29	30	31

SEPTEMBER 2024

S	M	T	W	T	F	S
1	2	3	4	5	6	7
8	9	10	11	12	13	14
15	16	17	18	19	20	21
22	23	24	25	26	27	28
29	30					

Week of August 18–24

"God began the work of our redemption in the Heart of Mary, given that it was through her fiat that the redemption began to come about."
SISTER LÚCIA

WEEKLY GOALS

HABIT TRACKER

S M T W T F S

THIS WEEK

MEAL PLAN

Sunday

Monday

Tuesday

Wednesday

Thursday

Friday

Saturday

THINGS TO REMEMBER

SUNDAY, AUGUST 18 / Thirteenth Sunday after Pentecost

MONDAY, AUGUST 19 / St. John Eudes

TUESDAY, AUGUST 20 / St. Bernard of Clairvaux

WEDNESDAY, AUGUST 21 / St. Jane Frances de Chantal

THURSDAY, AUGUST 22 / Immaculate Heart of the B.V.M.

FRIDAY, AUGUST 23 / St. Philip Benizi

SATURDAY, AUGUST 24 / St. Bartholomew the Apostle

CALL / EMAIL / FOLLOW-UP

AUGUST 2024

S	M	T	W	T	F	S
				1	2	3
4	5	6	7	8	9	10
11	12	13	14	15	16	17
18	19	20	21	22	23	24
25	26	27	28	29	30	31

SEPTEMBER 2024

S	M	T	W	T	F	S
1	2	3	4	5	6	7
8	9	10	11	12	13	14
15	16	17	18	19	20	21
22	23	24	25	26	27	28
29	30					

Week of August 25–31

"Do not be afraid to abandon yourself unreservedly to His loving Providence, for a child cannot perish in the arms of a Father Who is omnipotent."

ST. MARGARET MARY ALACOQUE

WEEKLY GOALS

HABIT TRACKER

S M T W T F S

THIS WEEK

MEAL PLAN

Sunday

Monday

Tuesday

Wednesday

Thursday

Friday

Saturday

THINGS TO REMEMBER

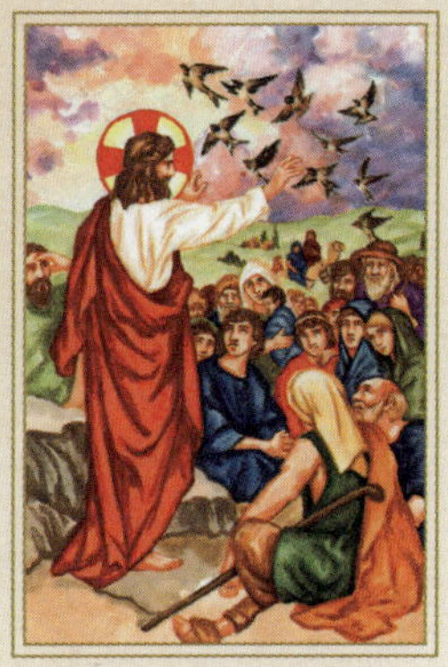

II **SUNDAY, AUGUST 25** / Fourteenth Sunday after Pentecost

- ☐
- ☐
- ☐
- ☐
- ☐
- ☐
- ☐
- ☐
- ☐

"Seek ye therefore first the kingdom of God, and his justice, and all these things shall be added unto you."

MATTHEW 6:33

IV **MONDAY, AUGUST 26** / Feria

- ☐
- ☐
- ☐
- ☐
- ☐
- ☐
- ☐
- ☐
- ☐
- ☐

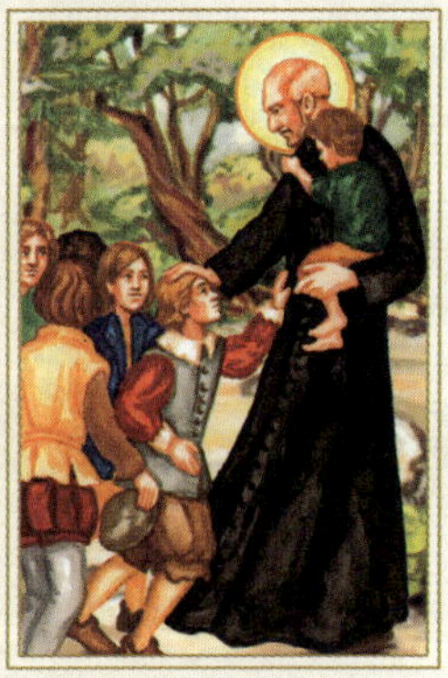

III **TUESDAY, AUGUST 27** / St. Joseph Calasance

- ☐
- ☐
- ☐
- ☐
- ☐
- ☐
- ☐
- ☐
- ☐
- ☐

III **WEDNESDAY, AUGUST 28** / St. Augustine

- ☐
- ☐
- ☐
- ☐
- ☐
- ☐
- ☐
- ☐
- ☐

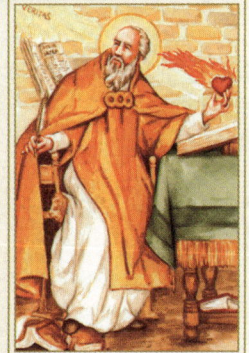

THURSDAY, AUGUST 29 / The Beheading of St. John the Baptist

FRIDAY, AUGUST 30 / St. Rose of Lima

SATURDAY, AUGUST 31 / St. Raymond Nonnatus

CALL / EMAIL / FOLLOW-UP

AUGUST 2024

S	M	T	W	T	F	S
				1	2	3
4	5	6	7	8	9	10
11	12	13	14	15	16	17
18	19	20	21	22	23	24
25	26	27	28	29	30	31

SEPTEMBER 2024

S	M	T	W	T	F	S
1	2	3	4	5	6	7
8	9	10	11	12	13	14
15	16	17	18	19	20	21
22	23	24	25	26	27	28
29	30					

September
The Month of the Seven Sorrows of Our Lady

I. The Prophecy of Simeon II. The Flight into Egypt III. The loss of the Child Jesus in the Temple IV. Mary meets Jesus on the way to Calvary V. The Crucifixion and Death of Jesus VI. Jesus is taken down from the Cross and laid in the arms of his mother VII. The Burial of Jesus

PRAYER FOR SEPTEMBER

O most holy Virgin, Mother of our Lord Jesus Christ, by the overwhelming grief you experienced when you witnessed the martyrdom, the crucifixion, and the death of your divine Son, look upon me with eyes of compassion, and awaken in my heart a tender commiseration for those sufferings.

—EXCERPT FROM A PRAYER TO OUR LADY OF SORROWS BY ST. BONAVENTURE

GOALS AND NOTES

September 2024
The Month of the Seven Sorrows of Our Lady

AUGUST 2024							OCTOBER 2024						
S	M	T	W	T	F	S	S	M	T	W	T	F	S
				1	2	3			1	2	3	4	5
4	5	6	7	8	9	10	6	7	8	9	10	11	12
11	12	13	14	15	16	17	13	14	15	16	17	18	19
18	19	20	21	22	23	24	20	21	22	23	24	25	26
25	26	27	28	29	30	31	27	28	29	30	31		

SUNDAY *Resurrection & Trinity*	MONDAY *Holy Spirit*	TUESDAY *Holy Angels*	WEDNESDAY *St. Joseph*
1 Fifteenth Sunday after Pentecost	**2** Labor Day St. Stephen of Hungary	**3** St. Pius X	**4**
8 Sixteenth Sunday after Pentecost	**9** St. Peter Claver	**10** St. Nicholas of Tolentino	**11**
15 Seventeenth Sunday after Pentecost	**16** Sts. Cornelius and Cyprian	**17**	**18** Ember Wednesday of September
22 Eighteenth Sunday after Pentecost	**23** St. Linus	**24**	**25**
29 THE DEDICATION OF ST. MICHAEL THE ARCHANGEL	**30** St. Jerome		

> "If you want to assist at Mass, with devotion and with fruit, think of the sorrowful Mother at the feet of Calvary."
>
> ST. PADRE PIO

THURSDAY *The Eucharist*	FRIDAY *Christ's Passion*	SATURDAY *The Blessed Virgin Mary*
5 St. Lawrence Justinian	**6**	**7**
12 The Most Holy Name of Mary	**13**	**14** The Exaltation of the Holy Cross
19 St. Januarius and Companions	**20** Ember Friday of September	**21** St. Matthew
26 Sts. Isaac Jogues, John de Brébeuf, and Companions	**27** Sts. Cosmas and Damian	**28** St. Wenceslaus

NOTES

Week of September 1–7

"The greatest obstacle in the apostolate of the Church is the timidity or rather the cowardice of the faithful."
ST. PIUS X

WEEKLY GOALS

- [ ]
- [ ]
- [ ]
- [ ]
- [ ]
- [ ]
- [ ]
- [ ]
- [ ]

HABIT TRACKER

	S	M	T	W	T	F	S
_____	○	○	○	○	○	○	○
_____	○	○	○	○	○	○	○
_____	○	○	○	○	○	○	○
_____	○	○	○	○	○	○	○
_____	○	○	○	○	○	○	○
_____	○	○	○	○	○	○	○
_____	○	○	○	○	○	○	○
_____	○	○	○	○	○	○	○

THIS WEEK

- [ ] ....
- [ ] ....
- [ ] ....
- [ ] ....
- [ ] ....
- [ ] ....
- [ ] ....
- [ ] ....
- [ ] ....
- [ ] ....
- [ ] ....
- [ ] ....
- [ ] ....
- [ ] ....
- [ ] ....
- [ ] ....
- [ ] ....
- [ ] ....
- [ ] ....

MEAL PLAN

Sunday

Monday

Tuesday

Wednesday

Thursday

Friday

Saturday

THINGS TO REMEMBER

....
....
....
....
....

II · SUNDAY, SEPTEMBER 1 / Fifteenth Sunday after Pentecost

III · MONDAY, SEPTEMBER 2 / St. Stephen of Hungary / Labor Day

III · TUESDAY, SEPTEMBER 3 / St. Pius X

"Whom when the Lord had seen, being moved with mercy towards her, he said to her: Weep not."

LUKE 7:13

IV · WEDNESDAY, SEPTEMBER 4 / Feria

THURSDAY, SEPTEMBER 5 / St. Lawrence Justinian

- [ ] ....
- [ ] ....
- [ ] ....
- [ ] ....
- [ ] ....
- [ ] ....
- [ ] ....
- [ ] ....
- [ ] ....
- [ ] ....

FRIDAY, SEPTEMBER 6 / Feria / *First Friday*

- [ ] ....
- [ ] ....
- [ ] ....
- [ ] ....
- [ ] ....
- [ ] ....
- [ ] ....
- [ ] ....
- [ ] ....
- [ ] ....

> "Incline thy ear, O Lord, and hear me: for I am needy and poor. Preserve my soul."
>
> **PSALMS 85:1–2**

SATURDAY, SEPTEMBER 7 / Our Lady on Saturday / *First Saturday*

- [ ] ....
- [ ] ....
- [ ] ....
- [ ] ....
- [ ] ....
- [ ] ....
- [ ] ....
- [ ] ....
- [ ] ....
- [ ] ....

CALL / EMAIL / FOLLOW-UP

SEPTEMBER 2024

S	M	T	W	T	F	S
1	2	3	4	5	6	7
8	9	10	11	12	13	14
15	16	17	18	19	20	21
22	23	24	25	26	27	28
29	30					

OCTOBER 2024

S	M	T	W	T	F	S
		1	2	3	4	5
6	7	8	9	10	11	12
13	14	15	16	17	18	19
20	21	22	23	24	25	26
27	28	29	30	31		

Week of September 8–14

"But far be it from me to glory except in the cross of our Lord Jesus Christ, by which the world has been crucified to me, and I to the world."
ST. PAUL THE APOSTLE

WEEKLY GOALS

HABIT TRACKER

S M T W T F S

THIS WEEK

MEAL PLAN

Sunday

Monday

Tuesday

Wednesday

Thursday

Friday

Saturday

THINGS TO REMEMBER

SUNDAY, SEPTEMBER 8 / Sixteenth Sunday after Pentecost

MONDAY, SEPTEMBER 9 / St. Peter Claver

TUESDAY, SEPTEMBER 10 / St. Nicholas of Tolentino

WEDNESDAY, SEPTEMBER 11 / Feria

"And Jesus answering, spoke to the lawyers and Pharisees, saying: Is it lawful to heal on the sabbath day?"

LUKE 14:3

THURSDAY, SEPTEMBER 12 / The Most Holy Name of Mary

FRIDAY, SEPTEMBER 13 / Feria

> "He hath so magnified thy name this day, that thy praise shall not depart out of the mouth of men."
>
> **JUDITH 13:25**

SATURDAY, SEPTEMBER 14 / The Exaltation of the Holy Cross

CALL / EMAIL / FOLLOW-UP

SEPTEMBER 2024

S	M	T	W	T	F	S
1	2	3	4	5	6	7
8	9	10	11	12	13	14
15	16	17	18	19	20	21
22	23	24	25	26	27	28
29	30					

OCTOBER 2024

S	M	T	W	T	F	S
		1	2	3	4	5
6	7	8	9	10	11	12
13	14	15	16	17	18	19
20	21	22	23	24	25	26
27	28	29	30	31		

Week of September 15–21

"O Lady, tell me, where didst thou stand? Was it only at the foot of the Cross? Ah, much more than this, thou wast on the Cross itself, crucified with thy Son."
ST. BONAVENTURE

WEEKLY GOALS

HABIT TRACKER

S M T W T F S

THIS WEEK

MEAL PLAN

Sunday

Monday

Tuesday

Wednesday

Thursday

Friday

Saturday

THINGS TO REMEMBER

II SUNDAY, SEPTEMBER 15 / Seventeenth Sunday after Pentecost

III MONDAY, SEPTEMBER 16 / Sts. Cornelius and Cyprian

> "Thou shalt love the Lord thy God with thy whole heart, and with thy whole soul, and with thy whole mind."
>
> MATTHEW 22:37

IV TUESDAY, SEPTEMBER 17 / Feria

II WEDNESDAY, SEPTEMBER 18 / Ember Wednesday of September

THURSDAY, SEPTEMBER 19 / St. Januarius and Companions

FRIDAY, SEPTEMBER 20 / Ember Friday of September

SATURDAY, SEPTEMBER 21 / St. Matthew

CALL / EMAIL / FOLLOW-UP

SEPTEMBER 2024

S	M	T	W	T	F	S
1	2	3	4	5	6	7
8	9	10	11	12	13	14
15	16	17	18	19	20	21
22	23	24	25	26	27	28
29	30					

OCTOBER 2024

S	M	T	W	T	F	S
		1	2	3	4	5
6	7	8	9	10	11	12
13	14	15	16	17	18	19
20	21	22	23	24	25	26
27	28	29	30	31		

Week of September 22–28

"Show me your hands. Do they have scars from giving? Show me your feet. Are they wounded in service? Show me your heart. Have you left a place for divine love?"

VEN. FULTON SHEEN

WEEKLY GOALS

HABIT TRACKER

S M T W T F S

THIS WEEK

MEAL PLAN

Sunday

Monday

Tuesday

Wednesday

Thursday

Friday

Saturday

THINGS TO REMEMBER

II SUNDAY, SEPTEMBER 22 / Eighteenth Sunday after Pentecost

- ☐ ....
- ☐ ....
- ☐ ....
- ☐ ....
- ☐ ....
- ☐ ....
- ☐ ....
- ☐ ....
- ☐ ....
- ☐ ....
- ☐ ....
- ☐ ....

III MONDAY, SEPTEMBER 23 / St. Linus

- ☐ ....
- ☐ ....
- ☐ ....
- ☐ ....
- ☐ ....
- ☐ ....
- ☐ ....
- ☐ ....
- ☐ ....
- ☐ ....
- ☐ ....
- ☐ ....

> "And the multitude seeing it, feared, and glorified God that gave such power to men."
> MATTHEW 9:8

IV TUESDAY, SEPTEMBER 24 / Feria

- ☐ ....
- ☐ ....
- ☐ ....
- ☐ ....
- ☐ ....
- ☐ ....
- ☐ ....
- ☐ ....
- ☐ ....
- ☐ ....
- ☐ ....
- ☐ ....

> "I rejoiced at the things that were said to me: We shall go into the house of the Lord."
> PSALMS 121:1

IV WEDNESDAY, SEPTEMBER 25 / Feria

- ☐ ....
- ☐ ....
- ☐ ....
- ☐ ....
- ☐ ....
- ☐ ....
- ☐ ....
- ☐ ....
- ☐ ....
- ☐ ....
- ☐ ....
- ☐ ....

THURSDAY, SEPTEMBER 26 / Sts. Isaac Jogues, John de Brébeuf, and Companions

FRIDAY, SEPTEMBER 27 / Sts. Cosmas and Damian

SATURDAY, SEPTEMBER 28 / St. Wenceslaus

CALL / EMAIL / FOLLOW-UP

SEPTEMBER 2024

S	M	T	W	T	F	S
1	2	3	4	5	6	7
8	9	10	11	12	13	14
15	16	17	18	19	20	21
22	23	24	25	26	27	28
29	30					

OCTOBER 2024

S	M	T	W	T	F	S
		1	2	3	4	5
6	7	8	9	10	11	12
13	14	15	16	17	18	19
20	21	22	23	24	25	26
27	28	29	30	31		

October

The Month of the Holy Rosary

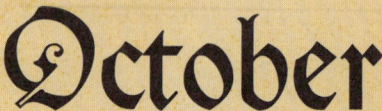

PRAYER FOR OCTOBER

Remember, O most gracious Virgin Mary, that never was it known that anyone who fled to thy protection, implored thy help, or sought thy intercession, was left unaided. Inspired with this confidence, I fly unto thee, O Virgin of virgins, my Mother. To thee do I come, before thee I stand, sinful and sorrowful. O Mother of the Word Incarnate, despise not my petitions, but in thy mercy, hear and answer me. Amen.

–THE MEMORARE

GOALS AND NOTES

October 2024

The Month of the Holy Rosary

SEPTEMBER 2024	NOVEMBER 2024
S M T W T F S	S M T W T F S
1 2 3 4 5 6 7	1 2
8 9 10 11 12 13 14	3 4 5 6 7 8 9
15 16 17 18 19 20 21	10 11 12 13 14 15 16
22 23 24 25 26 27 28	17 18 19 20 21 22 23
29 30	24 25 26 27 28 29 30

SUNDAY *Resurrection & Trinity*	MONDAY *Holy Spirit*	TUESDAY *Holy Angels*	WEDNESDAY *St. Joseph*
		1	**2** The Holy Guardian Angels
6 Twentieth Sunday after Pentecost	**7** Our Lady of the Rosary	**8** St. Bridget of Sweden	**9** St. John Leonard
13 Twenty-First Sunday after Pentecost	**14** Columbus Day St. Callistus I	**15** St. Teresa of Ávila	**16** St. Hedwig
20 Twenty-Second Sunday after Pentecost	**21**	**22**	**23** St. Anthony Mary Claret
27 CHRIST THE KING	**28** Sts. Simon and Jude	**29**	**30**

> "Never will anyone who says his Rosary every day be led astray. This is a statement that I would gladly sign with my blood."
>
> ST. LOUIS DE MONTFORT

THURSDAY *The Eucharist*	FRIDAY *Christ's Passion*	SATURDAY *The Blessed Virgin Mary*
3 St. Thérèse of Lisieux	**4** St. Francis of Assisi	**5**
10 St. Francis Borgia	**11** The Maternity of the B.V.M.	**12**
17 St. Margaret Mary Alacoque	**18** St. Luke the Evangelist	**19** St. Peter of Alcantara
24 St. Raphael the Archangel	**25** St. Isidore the Farm-Laborer	**26**
31 All Hallow's Eve		

NOTES

Week of September 29–October 5

"I take refuge, then, in prayer, and turn to Mary, and our Lord always triumphs."
ST. THÉRÈSE OF LISIEUX

WEEKLY GOALS

HABIT TRACKER

S M T W T F S

THIS WEEK

MEAL PLAN

Sunday

Monday

Tuesday

Wednesday

Thursday

Friday

Saturday

THINGS TO REMEMBER

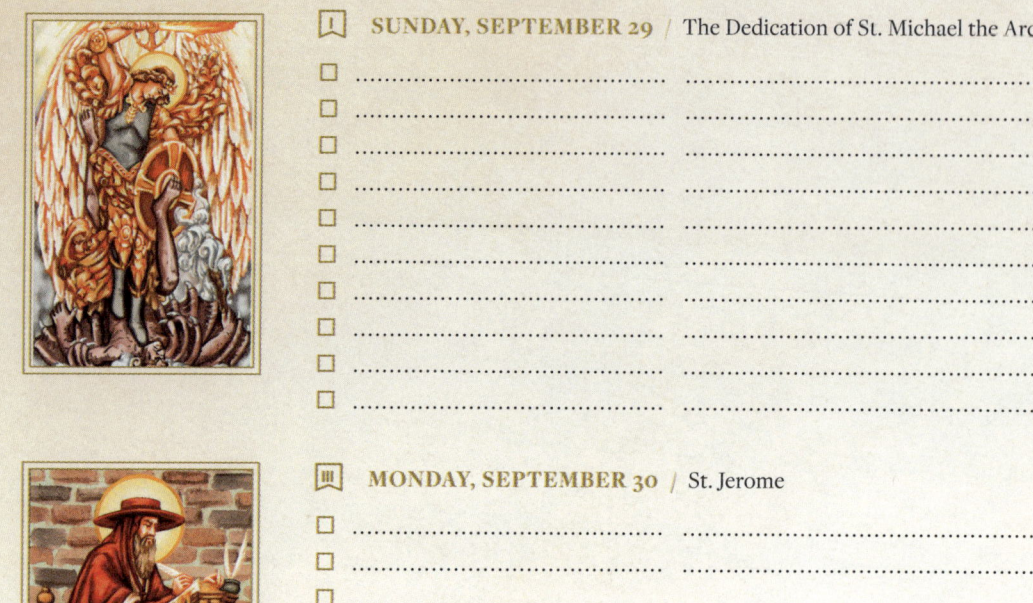

📖 **SUNDAY, SEPTEMBER 29** / The Dedication of St. Michael the Archangel

- [ ] ....
- [ ] ....
- [ ] ....
- [ ] ....
- [ ] ....
- [ ] ....
- [ ] ....
- [ ] ....
- [ ] ....
- [ ] ....

III MONDAY, SEPTEMBER 30 / St. Jerome

- [ ] ....
- [ ] ....
- [ ] ....
- [ ] ....
- [ ] ....
- [ ] ....
- [ ] ....
- [ ] ....
- [ ] ....
- [ ] ....

> "For he hath given his angels charge over thee; to keep thee in all thy ways."
>
> **PSALMS 90:11**

IV TUESDAY, OCTOBER 1 / Feria

- [ ] ....
- [ ] ....
- [ ] ....
- [ ] ....
- [ ] ....
- [ ] ....
- [ ] ....
- [ ] ....
- [ ] ....
- [ ] ....

III WEDNESDAY, OCTOBER 2 / The Holy Guardian Angels

- [ ] ....
- [ ] ....
- [ ] ....
- [ ] ....
- [ ] ....
- [ ] ....
- [ ] ....
- [ ] ....
- [ ] ....

THURSDAY, OCTOBER 3 / St. Thérèse of Lisieux

☐ ....
☐ ....
☐ ....
☐ ....
☐ ....
☐ ....
☐ ....
☐ ....
☐ ....
☐ ....
☐ ....

FRIDAY, OCTOBER 4 / St. Francis of Assisi / *First Friday*

☐ ....
☐ ....
☐ ....
☐ ....
☐ ....
☐ ....
☐ ....
☐ ....
☐ ....
☐ ....
☐ ....

SATURDAY, OCTOBER 5 / Our Lady on Saturday / *First Saturday*

☐ ....
☐ ....
☐ ....
☐ ....
☐ ....
☐ ....
☐ ....
☐ ....
☐ ....
☐ ....
☐ ....

CALL / EMAIL / FOLLOW-UP

OCTOBER 2024

S	M	T	W	T	F	S
		1	2	3	4	5
6	7	8	9	10	11	12
13	14	15	16	17	18	19
20	21	22	23	24	25	26
27	28	29	30	31		

NOVEMBER 2024

S	M	T	W	T	F	S
				1	2	3
4	5	6	7	8	9	10
11	12	13	14	15	16	17
18	19	20	21	22	23	24
25	26	27	28	29	30	

Week of October 6–12

"It seems unbelievable that a man should perish in whose favor Christ said to His Mother: 'Behold thy son,' provided that he has not turned a deaf ear to the words, which Christ addressed to him: 'Behold thy Mother.'"

ST. ROBERT BELLARMINE

WEEKLY GOALS

HABIT TRACKER

S M T W T F S

THIS WEEK

MEAL PLAN

- Sunday
- Monday
- Tuesday
- Wednesday
- Thursday
- Friday
- Saturday

THINGS TO REMEMBER

SUNDAY, OCTOBER 6 / Twentieth Sunday after Pentecost

MONDAY, OCTOBER 7 / Our Lady of the Rosary

TUESDAY, OCTOBER 8 / St. Bridget of Sweden

WEDNESDAY, OCTOBER 9 / St. John Leonard

THURSDAY, OCTOBER 10 / St. Francis Borgia

FRIDAY, OCTOBER 11 / The Maternity of the B.V.M.

SATURDAY, OCTOBER 12 / Our Lady on Saturday

CALL / EMAIL / FOLLOW-UP

OCTOBER 2024

S	M	T	W	T	F	S
		1	2	3	4	5
6	7	8	9	10	11	12
13	14	15	16	17	18	19
20	21	22	23	24	25	26
27	28	29	30	31		

NOVEMBER 2024

S	M	T	W	T	F	S
					1	2
3	4	5	6	7	8	9
10	11	12	13	14	15	16
17	18	19	20	21	22	23
24	25	26	27	28	29	30

Week of October 13–19

"The closer one approaches to God, the simpler one becomes."
ST. TERESA OF ÁVILA

WEEKLY GOALS

HABIT TRACKER

S M T W T F S

THIS WEEK

MEAL PLAN

Sunday

Monday

Tuesday

Wednesday

Thursday

Friday

Saturday

THINGS TO REMEMBER

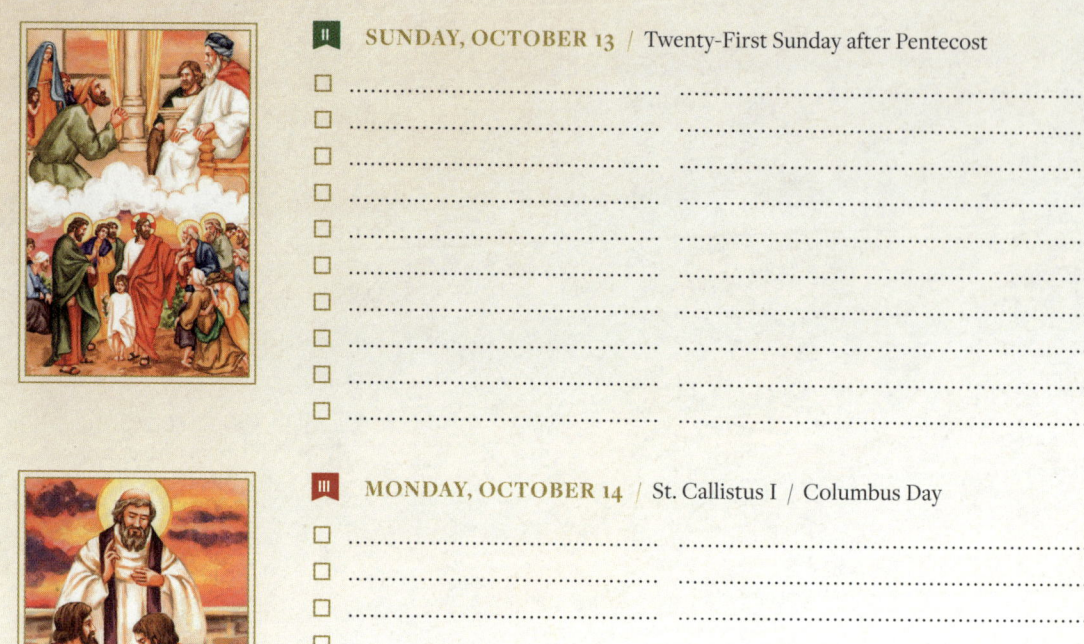

SUNDAY, OCTOBER 13 / Twenty-First Sunday after Pentecost

MONDAY, OCTOBER 14 / St. Callistus I / Columbus Day

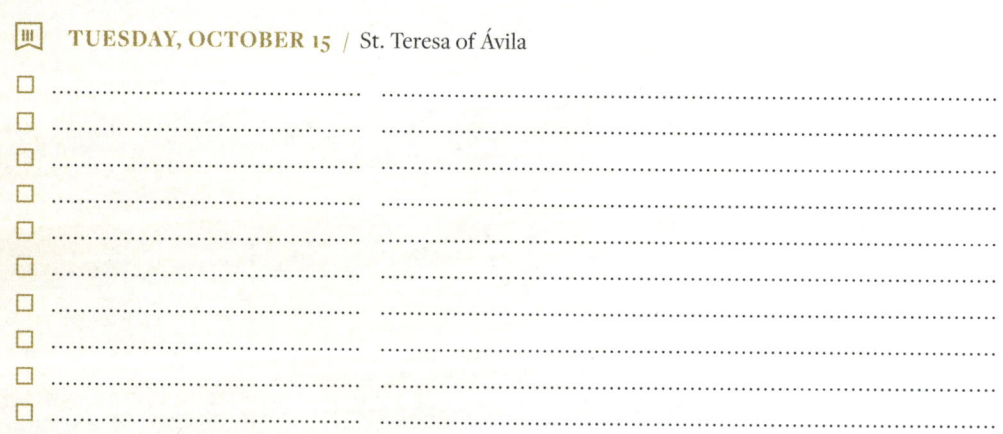

TUESDAY, OCTOBER 15 / St. Teresa of Ávila

WEDNESDAY, OCTOBER 16 / St. Hedwig

THURSDAY, OCTOBER 17 / St. Margaret Mary Alacoque

☐ ....
☐ ....
☐ ....
☐ ....
☐ ....
☐ ....
☐ ....
☐ ....
☐ ....
☐ ....

FRIDAY, OCTOBER 18 / St. Luke the Evangelist

☐ ....
☐ ....
☐ ....
☐ ....
☐ ....
☐ ....
☐ ....
☐ ....
☐ ....
☐ ....

SATURDAY, OCTOBER 19 / St. Peter of Alcantara

☐ ....
☐ ....
☐ ....
☐ ....
☐ ....
☐ ....
☐ ....
☐ ....
☐ ....
☐ ....

CALL / EMAIL / FOLLOW-UP

OCTOBER 2024

S	M	T	W	T	F	S
		1	2	3	4	5
6	7	8	9	10	11	12
13	14	15	16	17	18	19
20	21	22	23	24	25	26
27	28	29	30	31		

NOVEMBER 2024

S	M	T	W	T	F	S
					1	2
3	4	5	6	7	8	9
10	11	12	13	14	15	16
17	18	19	20	21	22	23
24	25	26	27	28	29	30

Week of October 20–26

"Christian perfection consists in three things: praying heroically, working heroically, and suffering heroically."
ST. ANTHONY MARY CLARET

WEEKLY GOALS

HABIT TRACKER

S M T W T F S

THIS WEEK

MEAL PLAN

Sunday

Monday

Tuesday

Wednesday

Thursday

Friday

Saturday

THINGS TO REMEMBER

II SUNDAY, OCTOBER 20 / Twenty-Second Sunday after Pentecost

IV MONDAY, OCTOBER 21 / Feria

"Render therefore to Caesar the things that are Caesar's; and to God, the things that are God's."

MATTHEW 22:21

IV TUESDAY, OCTOBER 22 / Feria

"If thou, O Lord, wilt mark iniquities: Lord, who shall stand it. For with thee there is merciful forgiveness."

PSALMS 129:3-4

III WEDNESDAY, OCTOBER 23 / St. Anthony Mary Claret

III · THURSDAY, OCTOBER 24 / St. Raphael the Archangel

- ☐ ....
- ☐ ....
- ☐ ....
- ☐ ....
- ☐ ....
- ☐ ....
- ☐ ....
- ☐ ....
- ☐ ....
- ☐ ....
- ☐ ....

III · FRIDAY, OCTOBER 25 / St. Isidore the Farm-Laborer

- ☐ ....
- ☐ ....
- ☐ ....
- ☐ ....
- ☐ ....
- ☐ ....
- ☐ ....
- ☐ ....
- ☐ ....
- ☐ ....
- ☐ ....

IV · SATURDAY, OCTOBER 26 / Our Lady on Saturday

- ☐ ....
- ☐ ....
- ☐ ....
- ☐ ....
- ☐ ....
- ☐ ....
- ☐ ....
- ☐ ....
- ☐ ....
- ☐ ....
- ☐ ....

CALL / EMAIL / FOLLOW-UP

OCTOBER 2024

S	M	T	W	T	F	S
		1	2	3	4	5
6	7	8	9	10	11	12
13	14	15	16	17	18	19
20	21	22	23	24	25	26
27	28	29	30	31		

NOVEMBER 2024

S	M	T	W	T	F	S
				1	2	3
4	5	6	7	8	9	10
11	12	13	14	15	16	17
18	19	20	21	22	23	24
25	26	27	28	29	30	

November

The Month of All Souls

PRAYER FOR NOVEMBER

Eternal rest grant unto them, O Lord, and let perpetual light shine upon them. May the souls of all the faithful departed, through the mercy of God, rest in peace. Amen.

–THE REQUIEM PRAYER

GOALS AND NOTES

November 2024

The Month of All Souls

OCTOBER 2024							DECEMBER 2024						
S	M	T	W	T	F	S	S	M	T	W	T	F	S
		1	2	3	4	5	1	2	3	4	5	6	7
6	7	8	9	10	11	12	8	9	10	11	12	13	14
13	14	15	16	17	18	19	15	16	17	18	19	20	21
20	21	22	23	24	25	26	22	23	24	25	26	27	28
27	28	29	30	31			29	30	31				

SUNDAY *Resurrection & Trinity*	MONDAY *Holy Spirit*	TUESDAY *Holy Angels*	WEDNESDAY *St. Joseph*
3 Daylight Saving Time ends Fourth Resumed Sunday after Epiphany	**4** St. Charles Borromeo	**5**	**6**
10 Fifth Resumed Sunday after Epiphany	**11** Veterans Day St. Martin of Tours	**12** St. Martin I	**13** St. Frances Xavier Cabrini
17 Sixth Resumed Sunday after Epiphany	**18** The Dedication of the Basilicas of Sts. Peter and Paul	**19** St. Elizabeth of Hungary	**20** St. Felix of Valois
24 Twenty-Fourth and Last Sunday after Pentecost	**25** St. Catherine of Alexandria	**26** St. Sylvester Gozzolini	**27**

> "He who saves a soul saves his own and satisfies for a multitude of sins."
> ST. JAMES THE APOSTLE

THURSDAY *The Eucharist*	FRIDAY *Christ's Passion*	SATURDAY *The Blessed Virgin Mary*
	1 ALL SAINTS *Holy Day of Obligation*	2 **ALL SOULS**
7	8	9 The Dedication of the Archbasilica of the Most Holy Savior
14 St. Josaphat Kuntsevych	15 St. Albert the Great	16 St. Gertrude the Great
21 The Presentation of the B.V.M.	22 St. Cecilia	23 St. Clement I
28 Thanksgiving (USA)	29	30 **St. Andrew the Apostle**

NOTES

Week of October 27–November 2

"The last judgment shall fill sinners with terror, but will be a source of joy and sweetness to the elect; for the Lord will then give praise to each one according to his works."

ST. ALPHONSUS MARY OF LIGUORI

WEEKLY GOALS

HABIT TRACKER

S M T W T F S

THIS WEEK

MEAL PLAN

Sunday

Monday

Tuesday

Wednesday

Thursday

Friday

Saturday

THINGS TO REMEMBER

SUNDAY, OCTOBER 27 / Christ the King

MONDAY, OCTOBER 28 / Sts. Simon and Jude

> "The Lord shall sit king for ever. The Lord will give strength to his people: the Lord will bless his people with peace."
>
> PSALMS 28:10

TUESDAY, OCTOBER 29 / Feria

> "Fear the Lord, all ye his saints: for there is no want to them that fear him."
>
> PSALMS 33:10

WEDNESDAY, OCTOBER 30 / Feria

THURSDAY, OCTOBER 31 / Feria / All Hallow's Eve

- [ ] ....
- [ ] ....
- [ ] ....
- [ ] ....
- [ ] ....
- [ ] ....
- [ ] ....
- [ ] ....
- [ ] ....
- [ ] ....

> "The hour cometh, and now is, when the dead shall hear the voice of the Son of God, and they that hear shall live."
>
> **JOHN 5:25**

FRIDAY, NOVEMBER 1 / All Saints / *Holy Day of Obligation* / *First Friday*

- [ ] ....
- [ ] ....
- [ ] ....
- [ ] ....
- [ ] ....
- [ ] ....
- [ ] ....
- [ ] ....
- [ ] ....
- [ ] ....

SATURDAY, NOVEMBER 2 / All Souls / *First Saturday*

- [ ] ....
- [ ] ....
- [ ] ....
- [ ] ....
- [ ] ....
- [ ] ....
- [ ] ....
- [ ] ....
- [ ] ....
- [ ] ....

CALL / EMAIL / FOLLOW-UP

NOVEMBER 2024

S	M	T	W	T	F	S
					1	2
3	4	5	6	7	8	9
10	11	12	13	14	15	16
17	18	19	20	21	22	23
24	25	26	27	28	29	30

DECEMBER 2024

S	M	T	W	T	F	S
1	2	3	4	5	6	7
8	9	10	11	12	13	14
15	16	17	18	19	20	21
22	23	24	25	26	27	28
29	30	31				

Week of November 3–9

"Do not have any anxiety about the future. Leave everything in God's hands for He will take care of you."
ST. JEAN-BAPTISTE DE LA SALLE

WEEKLY GOALS

HABIT TRACKER

S M T W T F S

THIS WEEK

MEAL PLAN

Sunday

Monday

Tuesday

Wednesday

Thursday

Friday

Saturday

THINGS TO REMEMBER

SUNDAY, NOVEMBER 3 / Fourth Resumed Sunday after Epiphany / Daylight Saving Time Ends

MONDAY, NOVEMBER 4 / St. Charles Borromeo

"Why are you fearful, O ye of little faith? Then rising up he commanded the winds, and the sea, and there came a great calm."

MATTHEW 8:26

TUESDAY, NOVEMBER 5 / Feria

"The right hand of the Lord hath wrought strength: the right hand of the Lord hath exulted me."

PSALMS 117:16

WEDNESDAY, NOVEMBER 6 / Feria

IV THURSDAY, NOVEMBER 7 / Feria

> "The heavens declared his justice: and all people saw his glory"
>
> **PSALMS 96:6**

IV FRIDAY, NOVEMBER 8 / Feria

> "The love of our neighbour worketh no evil. Love therefore is the fulfilling of the law."
>
> **ROMANS 13:10**

II SATURDAY, NOVEMBER 9 / The Dedication of the Archbasilica of the Most Holy Savior

---

CALL / EMAIL / FOLLOW-UP

NOVEMBER 2024

S	M	T	W	T	F	S
				1	2	3
4	5	6	7	8	9	10
11	12	13	14	15	16	17
18	19	20	21	22	23	24
25	26	27	28	29	30	

DECEMBER 2024

S	M	T	W	T	F	S
1	2	3	4	5	6	7
8	9	10	11	12	13	14
15	16	17	18	19	20	21
22	23	24	25	26	27	28
29	30	31				

Week of November 10–16

"I have served you as a soldier, now let me serve Christ."
ST. MARTIN OF TOURS

WEEKLY GOALS

HABIT TRACKER

S M T W T F S

THIS WEEK

MEAL PLAN

Sunday

Monday

Tuesday

Wednesday

Thursday

Friday

Saturday

THINGS TO REMEMBER

SUNDAY, NOVEMBER 10 / Fifth Resumed Sunday after Epiphany

MONDAY, NOVEMBER 11 / St. Martin of Tours / Veterans Day

TUESDAY, NOVEMBER 12 / St. Martin I

WEDNESDAY, NOVEMBER 13 / St. Frances Xavier Cabrini

THURSDAY, NOVEMBER 14 / St. Josaphat Kuntsevych

FRIDAY, NOVEMBER 15 / St. Albert the Great

SATURDAY, NOVEMBER 16 / St. Gertrude the Great

CALL / EMAIL / FOLLOW-UP

NOVEMBER 2024

S	M	T	W	T	F	S
				1	2	3
4	5	6	7	8	9	10
11	12	13	14	15	16	17
18	19	20	21	22	23	24
25	26	27	28	29	30	

DECEMBER 2024

S	M	T	W	T	F	S
1	2	3	4	5	6	7
8	9	10	11	12	13	14
15	16	17	18	19	20	21
22	23	24	25	26	27	28
29	30	31				

Week of November 17–23

"Follow the saints, because those who follow them will become saints."
POPE CLEMENT I

WEEKLY GOALS

HABIT TRACKER

S M T W T F S

THIS WEEK

MEAL PLAN

Sunday

Monday

Tuesday

Wednesday

Thursday

Friday

Saturday

THINGS TO REMEMBER

SUNDAY, NOVEMBER 17 / Sixth Resumed Sunday after Epiphany

MONDAY, NOVEMBER 18 / The Dedication of the Basilicas of Sts. Peter and Paul

TUESDAY, NOVEMBER 19 / St. Elizabeth of Hungary

WEDNESDAY, NOVEMBER 20 / St. Felix of Valois

THURSDAY, NOVEMBER 21 / The Presentation of the B.V.M.

FRIDAY, NOVEMBER 22 / St. Cecilia

SATURDAY, NOVEMBER 23 / St. Clement I

CALL / EMAIL / FOLLOW-UP

NOVEMBER 2024

S	M	T	W	T	F	S
					1	2
3	4	5	6	7	8	9
10	11	12	13	14	15	16
17	18	19	20	21	22	23
24	25	26	27	28	29	30

DECEMBER 2024

S	M	T	W	T	F	S
1	2	3	4	5	6	7
8	9	10	11	12	13	14
15	16	17	18	19	20	21
22	23	24	25	26	27	28
29	30	31				

Week of November 24–30

"And when the Son of man shall come in his majesty, and all the angels with him, then shall he sit upon the seat of his majesty. And all nations shall be gathered together before him."

MATTHEW 25:31-32

WEEKLY GOALS

- [ ]
- [ ]
- [ ]
- [ ]
- [ ]
- [ ]
- [ ]
- [ ]

HABIT TRACKER

	S	M	T	W	T	F	S
_____	○	○	○	○	○	○	○
_____	○	○	○	○	○	○	○
_____	○	○	○	○	○	○	○
_____	○	○	○	○	○	○	○
_____	○	○	○	○	○	○	○
_____	○	○	○	○	○	○	○
_____	○	○	○	○	○	○	○
_____	○	○	○	○	○	○	○

THIS WEEK

- [ ]
- [ ]
- [ ]
- [ ]
- [ ]
- [ ]
- [ ]
- [ ]
- [ ]
- [ ]
- [ ]
- [ ]
- [ ]
- [ ]
- [ ]
- [ ]
- [ ]
- [ ]
- [ ]
- [ ]

MEAL PLAN

Sunday

Monday

Tuesday

Wednesday

Thursday

Friday

Saturday

THINGS TO REMEMBER

II SUNDAY, NOVEMBER 24 / Twenty-Fourth and Last Sunday after Pentecost

III MONDAY, NOVEMBER 25 / St. Catherine of Alexandria

IIII TUESDAY, NOVEMBER 26 / St. Sylvester Gozzolini

"For there shall be then great tribulation, such as hath not been from the beginning of the world until now, neither shall be."

MATTHEW 24:21

IV WEDNESDAY, NOVEMBER 27 / Feria

IV THURSDAY, NOVEMBER 28 / Feria / Thanksgiving (USA)

> "And you shall call upon me, and you shall go: and you shall pray to me, and I will hear you."
>
> **JEREMIAH 29:12**

IV FRIDAY, NOVEMBER 29 / Feria

> "In God shall we glory all the day long: and in thy name we will give praise for ever."
>
> **PSALMS 43:9**

II SATURDAY, NOVEMBER 30 / St. Andrew the Apostle

CALL / EMAIL / FOLLOW-UP

NOVEMBER 2024

S	M	T	W	T	F	S
				1	2	3	4
5	6	7	8	9	10	11
12	13	14	15	16	17	18
19	20	21	22	23	24	25
26	27	28	29	30		

DECEMBER 2024

S	M	T	W	T	F	S
1	2	3	4	5	6	7
8	9	10	11	12	13	14
15	16	17	18	19	20	21
22	23	24	25	26	27	28
29	30	31				

December

The Month of the Immaculate Conception

PRAYER FOR DECEMBER

O Virgin, most pure, wholly unspotted, O Mary, Mother of God, Queen of the universe, You are above all the Saints, the hope of the elect and the joy of all the blessed. It is you who have reconciled us with God. You are the only refuge of sinners and the safe harbor of those who are shipwrecked. You are the consolation of the world, the ransom of captives, the health of the weak, the joy of the afflicted, and the salvation of all.

—EXCERPT FROM A PRAYER BY ST. EPHRAEM OF SYRIA

GOALS AND NOTES

December 2024
The Month of the Immaculate Conception

NOVEMBER 2024

S	M	T	W	T	F	S
					1	2
3	4	5	6	7	8	9
10	11	12	13	14	15	16
17	18	19	20	21	22	23
24	25	26	27	28	29	30

JANUARY 2025

S	M	T	W	T	F	S
			1	2	3	4
5	6	7	8	9	10	11
12	13	14	15	16	17	18
19	20	21	22	23	24	25
26	27	28	29	30	31	

SUNDAY *Resurrection & Trinity*	MONDAY *Holy Spirit*	TUESDAY *Holy Angels*	WEDNESDAY *St. Joseph*
1 **FIRST SUNDAY OF ADVENT**	**2** St. Bibiana	**3** St. Francis Xavier	**4** St. Peter Chrysologus
8 **THE IMMACULATE CONCEPTION**	**9**	**10**	**11** St. Damasus I
15 **THIRD SUNDAY OF ADVENT (GAUDETE SUNDAY)**	**16** St. Eusebius of Vercelli	**17** Greater Feria of Advent	**18** Ember Wednesday of Advent
22 **FOURTH SUNDAY OF ADVENT**	**23** Greater Feria of Advent	**24** **VIGIL OF THE NATIVITY**	**25** **THE NATIVITY OF OUR LORD** *Holy Day of Obligation*
29 Sunday in the Octave of Christmas	**30** Sixth Day in the Octave of Christmas	**31** New Year's Eve Seventh Day in the Octave of Christmas	

"Thou alone and Thy Mother are in all things fair; there is no flaw in Thee and no stain in Thy Mother."

ST. EPHREM OF SYRIA

THURSDAY *The Eucharist*	FRIDAY *Christ's Passion*	SATURDAY *The Blessed Virgin Mary*
5	6 St. Nicholas	7 St. Ambrose
12 Our Lady of Guadalupe	13 St. Lucy	14
19 **Greater Feria of Advent**	20 **Ember Friday of Advent**	21 **St. Thomas**
26 **St. Stephen**	27 **St. John the Evangelist**	28 **The Holy Innocents**

NOTES

Week of December 1–7

"May each one of us glorify the Lord with the soul of Mary and rejoice in God with the spirit of Mary."
ST. AMBROSE

WEEKLY GOALS

HABIT TRACKER

S M T W T F S

THIS WEEK

MEAL PLAN

Sunday

Monday

Tuesday

Wednesday

Thursday

Friday

Saturday

THINGS TO REMEMBER

I **SUNDAY, DECEMBER 1** / First Sunday of Advent

III **MONDAY, DECEMBER 2** / St. Bibiana

III **TUESDAY, DECEMBER 3** / St. Francis Xavier

III **WEDNESDAY, DECEMBER 4** / St. Peter Chrysologus

THURSDAY, DECEMBER 5 / Feria

> "When you shall see these things come to pass, know that the kingdom of God is at hand."
>
> LUKE 21:31

FRIDAY, DECEMBER 6 / St. Nicholas / *First Friday*

SATURDAY, DECEMBER 7 / St. Ambrose / *First Saturday*

CALL / EMAIL / FOLLOW-UP

DECEMBER 2024

S	M	T	W	T	F	S
1	2	3	4	5	6	7
8	9	10	11	12	13	14
15	16	17	18	19	20	21
22	23	24	25	26	27	28
29	30	31				

JANUARY 2025

S	M	T	W	T	F	S
			1	2	3	4
5	6	7	8	9	10	11
12	13	14	15	16	17	18
19	20	21	22	23	24	25
26	27	28	29	30	31	

Week of December 8–14

"Know and understand well, you my most humble son, that I am the ever-virgin Holy Mary, Mother of the True God for Whom we live, of the Creator of all things, Lord of Heaven and the earth."

OUR LADY OF GUADALUPE

WEEKLY GOALS

HABIT TRACKER

S M T W T F S

THIS WEEK

MEAL PLAN

Sunday

Monday

Tuesday

Wednesday

Thursday

Friday

Saturday

THINGS TO REMEMBER

SUNDAY, DECEMBER 8 / The Immaculate Conception

"Thou art all fair, O my love, and there is not a spot in thee."
CANTICLES 4:7

MONDAY, DECEMBER 9 / Feria

"He hath clothed me with the garments of salvation: and with the robe of justice he hath covered me."
ISAIAH 61:10

TUESDAY, DECEMBER 10 / Feria

WEDNESDAY, DECEMBER 11 / St. Damasus I

THURSDAY, DECEMBER 12 / Our Lady of Guadalupe

FRIDAY, DECEMBER 13 / St Lucy

SATURDAY, DECEMBER 14 / Feria

CALL / EMAIL / FOLLOW-UP

> "A great sign appeared in heaven: A woman clothed with the sun, and the moon under her feet, and on her head a crown of twelve stars."
>
> **REVELATION 12:1**

DECEMBER 2024

S	M	T	W	T	F	S
1	2	3	4	5	6	7
8	9	10	11	12	13	14
15	16	17	18	19	20	21
22	23	24	25	26	27	28
29	30	31				

JANUARY 2025

S	M	T	W	T	F	S
			1	2	3	4
5	6	7	8	9	10	11
12	13	14	15	16	17	18
19	20	21	22	23	24	25
26	27	28	29	30	31	

Week of December 15–21

"There hath stood one in the midst of you, whom you know not. The same is he that shall come after me, who is preferred before me: the latchet of whose shoe I am not worthy to loose."
JOHN 1:26–27

WEEKLY GOALS

HABIT TRACKER

S M T W T F S

THIS WEEK

MEAL PLAN

Sunday

Monday

Tuesday

Wednesday

Thursday

Friday

Saturday

THINGS TO REMEMBER

I SUNDAY, DECEMBER 15 / Third Sunday of Advent, Gaudete Sunday

☐ ....
☐ ....
☐ ....
☐ ....
☐ ....
☐ ....
☐ ....
☐ ....
☐ ....
☐ ....

III MONDAY, DECEMBER 16 / St. Eusebius of Vercelli

☐ ....
☐ ....
☐ ....
☐ ....
☐ ....
☐ ....
☐ ....
☐ ....
☐ ....
☐ ....

> "Wisdom shall praise her own self, and shall be honoured in God, and shall glory in the midst of her people."
> — SIRACH 24:1

II TUESDAY, DECEMBER 17 / Greater Feria of Advent (O Sapientia)

☐ ....
☐ ....
☐ ....
☐ ....
☐ ....
☐ ....
☐ ....
☐ ....
☐ ....
☐ ....

II WEDNESDAY, DECEMBER 18 / Ember Wednesday of Advent (O Adonai)

☐ ....
☐ ....
☐ ....
☐ ....
☐ ....
☐ ....
☐ ....
☐ ....
☐ ....
☐ ....

THURSDAY, DECEMBER 19 / Greater Feria of Advent (O Radix Jesse)

- [ ] ....
- [ ] ....
- [ ] ....
- [ ] ....
- [ ] ....
- [ ] ....
- [ ] ....
- [ ] ....
- [ ] ....
- [ ] ....

> "In that day the root of Jesse, who standeth for an ensign of the people, him the Gentiles shall beseech."
>
> ISAIAH 11:10

FRIDAY, DECEMBER 20 / Ember Friday of Advent (O Clavis David)

- [ ] ....
- [ ] ....
- [ ] ....
- [ ] ....
- [ ] ....
- [ ] ....
- [ ] ....
- [ ] ....
- [ ] ....
- [ ] ....

SATURDAY, DECEMBER 21 / St. Thomas (O Oriens)

- [ ] ....
- [ ] ....
- [ ] ....
- [ ] ....
- [ ] ....
- [ ] ....
- [ ] ....
- [ ] ....
- [ ] ....
- [ ] ....

CALL / EMAIL / FOLLOW-UP

DECEMBER 2024

S	M	T	W	T	F	S
1	2	3	4	5	6	7
8	9	10	11	12	13	14
15	16	17	18	19	20	21
22	23	24	25	26	27	28
29	30	31				

JANUARY 2025

S	M	T	W	T	F	S
			1	2	3	4
5	6	7	8	9	10	11
12	13	14	15	16	17	18
19	20	21	22	23	24	25
26	27	28	29	30	31	

Week of December 22–28

"That the Creator is in his creature and God is in the flesh brings dignity to man without dishonor to Him Who made him. Why then, man, are you so worthless in your own eyes and yet so precious to God?"
ST. PETER CHRYSOLOGUS

WEEKLY GOALS

HABIT TRACKER

S M T W T F S

THIS WEEK

MEAL PLAN

Sunday

Monday

Tuesday

Wednesday

Thursday

Friday

Saturday

THINGS TO REMEMBER

SUNDAY, DECEMBER 22 / Fourth Sunday of Advent (O Rex Gentium)

> "Behold a virgin shall conceive, and bear a son, and his name shall be called Emmanuel."
>
> ISAIAH 7:14

MONDAY, DECEMBER 23 / Greater Feria of Advent (O Emmanuel)

TUESDAY, DECEMBER 24 / Vigil of the Nativity

WEDNESDAY, DECEMBER 25 / The Nativity of Our Lord / *Holy Day of Obligation*

THURSDAY, DECEMBER 26 / St. Stephen

FRIDAY, DECEMBER 27 / St. John the Evangelist

SATURDAY, DECEMBER 28 / The Holy Innocents

CALL / EMAIL / FOLLOW-UP

DECEMBER 2024

S	M	T	W	T	F	S
1	2	3	4	5	6	7
8	9	10	11	12	13	14
15	16	17	18	19	20	21
22	23	24	25	26	27	28
29	30	31				

JANUARY 2025

S	M	T	W	T	F	S
			1	2	3	4
5	6	7	8	9	10	11
12	13	14	15	16	17	18
19	20	21	22	23	24	25
26	27	28	29	30	31	

Week of December 29–January 4

"The Magi are filled with awe by what they see; Heaven on earth and earth in Heaven; man in God and God in man; they see enclosed in a tiny body the One Whom the entire world cannot contain."

ST. PETER CHRYSOLOGUS

WEEKLY GOALS

HABIT TRACKER

S M T W T F S

THIS WEEK

MEAL PLAN

Sunday

Monday

Tuesday

Wednesday

Thursday

Friday

Saturday

THINGS TO REMEMBER

"For a CHILD IS BORN to us, and a son is given to us, and the government is upon his shoulder."

ISAIAH 9:6

"The Lord hath made known his salvation: he hath revealed his justice in the sight of the Gentiles."

PSALMS 97:2

SUNDAY, DECEMBER 29 / Sunday in the Octave of Christmas

MONDAY, DECEMBER 30 / Sixth Day in the Octave of Christmas

TUESDAY, DECEMBER 31 / Seventh Day in the Octave of Christmas / New Year's Eve

WEDNESDAY, JANUARY 1 / The Circumcision / New Year's Day / *Holy Day of Obligation*

THURSDAY, JANUARY 2 / Holy Name of Jesus

FRIDAY, JANUARY 3 / Feria of Christmas / *First Friday*

> "O Lord our Lord, how admirable is thy name in the whole earth! For thy magnificence is elevated above the heavens."
>
> PSALMS 8:2

SATURDAY, JANUARY 4 / Our Lady on Saturday / *First Saturday*

CALL / EMAIL / FOLLOW-UP

DECEMBER 2024

S	M	T	W	T	F	S
1	2	3	4	5	6	7
8	9	10	11	12	13	14
15	16	17	18	19	20	21
22	23	24	25	26	27	28
29	30	31				

JANUARY 2025

S	M	T	W	T	F	S
			1	2	3	4
5	6	7	8	9	10	11
12	13	14	15	16	17	18
19	20	21	22	23	24	25
26	27	28	29	30	31	

Future Planning

JANUARY 2025

S	M	T	W	T	F	S
			1	2	3	4
5	6	7	8	9	10	11
12	13	14	15	16	17	18
19	20	21	22	23	24	25
26	27	28	29	30	31	

FEBRUARY 2025

S	M	T	W	T	F	S
						1
2	3	4	5	6	7	8
9	10	11	12	13	14	15
16	17	18	19	20	21	22
23	24	25	26	27	28	

MARCH 2025

S	M	T	W	T	F	S
						1
2	3	4	5	6	7	8
9	10	11	12	13	14	15
16	17	18	19	20	21	22
23	24	25	26	27	28	29
30	31					

APRIL 2025

S	M	T	W	T	F	S
		1	2	3	4	5
6	7	8	9	10	11	12
13	14	15	16	17	18	19
20	21	22	23	24	25	26
27	28	29	30			

MAY 2025

S	M	T	W	T	F	S
				1	2	3
4	5	6	7	8	9	10
11	12	13	14	15	16	17
18	19	20	21	22	23	24
25	26	27	28	29	30	31

JUNE 2025

S	M	T	W	T	F	S
1	2	3	4	5	6	7
8	9	10	11	12	13	14
15	16	17	18	19	20	21
22	23	24	25	26	27	28
29	30					

Future Planning

JULY 2025

S	M	T	W	T	F	S
		1	2	3	4	5
6	7	8	9	10	11	12
13	14	15	16	17	18	19
20	21	22	23	24	25	26
27	28	29	30	31		

AUGUST 2025

S	M	T	W	T	F	S
					1	2
3	4	5	6	7	8	9
10	11	12	13	14	15	16
17	18	19	20	21	22	23
24	25	26	27	28	29	30
31						

SEPTEMBER 2025

S	M	T	W	T	F	S
	1	2	3	4	5	6
7	8	9	10	11	12	13
14	15	16	17	18	19	20
21	22	23	24	25	26	27
28	29	30				

OCTOBER 2025

S	M	T	W	T	F	S
			1	2	3	4
5	6	7	8	9	10	11
12	13	14	15	16	17	18
19	20	21	22	23	24	25
26	27	28	29	30	31	

NOVEMBER 2025

S	M	T	W	T	F	S
						1
2	3	4	5	6	7	8
9	10	11	12	13	14	15
16	17	18	19	20	21	22
23	24	25	26	27	28	29
30						

DECEMBER 2025

S	M	T	W	T	F	S
	1	2	3	4	5	6
7	8	9	10	11	12	13
14	15	16	17	18	19	20
21	22	23	24	25	26	27
28	29	30	31			

NOTES